# Power
## *through*
## Surrender

A Personal Pathway to Andrew
Murray's book Absolute Surrender

CHRIS BORSZCZ *and* LISA DAHLQUIST

WESTBOW
PRESS®
A DIVISION OF THOMAS NELSON
& ZONDERVAN

WestBow Press books may be ordered through booksellers or by contacting:

WestBow Press
A Division of Thomas Nelson & Zondervan
1663 Liberty Drive
Bloomington, IN 47403
www.westbowpress.com
844-714-3454

Unless otherwise indicated, all Scripture taken from the New King James Version®. Copyright © 1982 by Thomas Nelson. Used by permission. All rights reserved.

Scripture marked (KJV) taken from the King James Version of the Bible.

All original text from Absolute Surrender by Andrew Murray, Las Vegas, NV: Pantianos Classics, 2021, 1897 and Absolute Surrender by Andrew Murray, London & Edinburgh, Marshall, Morgan and Scott, First Edition, 1932.

ISBN: 978-1-6642-7914-8 (sc)
ISBN: 978-1-6642-7915-5 (hc)
ISBN: 978-1-6642-7913-1 (e)

Library of Congress Control Number: 2022917827

Print information available on the last page.

WestBow Press rev. date: 11/23/2022

# CONTENTS

# DEDICATIONS

We would like to give a special dedication to someone dear to our hearts.
She recognized our commitment to the Lord, put us behind a
podium, and told us we could teach the Word of God by surrendering
to Him. Thank you Lenya Heitzig, for giving us our foundation
in Christian ministry. We are eternally grateful to you.

To the loves of my life:
Tony, Mandy, Teresa, and Dan.
My grandgirls: June and Brookie

And to the love of my life: Phil

Last but not least to the two women who believed in me:
My Mother, June, and my co-author, Lisa

And the two best friends, who never left my side:
Gussy, my Pug and Lily, my Pomeranian

To the loves of my life in this world:
Erik and Will

To my dear friends, mentors, and prayer partners:
Betty Ann and Lisa B.

To my dear friend and co-writer:
Chris

May ALL Glory be to our Father in Heaven and Jesus
Christ along with His gift of the Holy Spirit!

# PREFACE

Andrew Murray's book, *Absolute Surrender*, was originally published in 1897. He spent 60 years in ministry in South Africa and published more than 200 Christian books and tracts. According to Christianity Today, Mr. Murray's continuous prayer was, "May not a single moment of my life be spent outside the light, love, and joy of God's presence. And not a moment without the entire surrender of myself as a vessel for him to fill full of his Spirit and his love." Truly, "casting himself on Christ" was the theme of Mr. Murray's life.[1]

Mr. Murray's book, *Absolute Surrender,* has had a tremendous impact on both our lives launching us onto a path of inexpressible closeness with the Lord and blessings unspeakable. This is due to absolutely surrendering all to Jesus Christ. Our deep desire is that you can enjoy these same blessings in your life. We trust that Jesus has prepared your heart for this exciting adventure for He knew you would be reading these words at this exact moment and "for such a time as this" in your life. God has your own personal pathway to absolute surrender open before you. Take His hand and follow where He leads.

# INTRODUCTION

It is our desire by God's grace to give you the truths of God's Word concerning absolute surrender previously taught and written by Andrew Murray in the late 1800's. Our intention is that this book would act as a guide to encourage and assist you on your personal journey of absolute surrender to God, as it did for us.

The text is written as close to Andrew Murray's original writings as possible, while changing some verbiage, sentences, etc. for clarity and to reflect the modern day usage of words. Also, at the end of each chapter we have included a section called, "Points to Ponder", which was not in Mr. Murray's writings.

We pray that in this book you will sense the Lord's Presence, be overwhelmed with His Love, thirst for more of Him, and see Him move in your life in ways you never dreamed possible. He loves you more than you know! It's going to be a fabulous journey! Let's begin…

# CHAPTER 1

## *What the Church and Believers Need Most: Absolute Surrender*

Now Ben-Hadad the king of Syria gathered all his forces together; thirty-two kings were with him, with horses and chariots. And he went up and besieged Samaria, and made war against it. Then he sent messengers into the city to Ahab, king of Israel, and said to him, "Thus says Ben-Hadad: 'Your silver and your gold are mine; your loveliest wives and children are mine.' And the king of Israel answered and said, 'My lord, O king, just as you say, I and all that I have are yours.'" 1 Kings 20:1-4

AHAB GAVE WHAT WAS ASKED OF HIM BY BEN-HADAD - ABSOLUTE SURRENDER. His words were, "My lord, O king, just as you say, I and all that I have are yours." May these be the words of absolute surrender spoken by every child of God as he yields himself to his Heavenly Father. If Ahab was willing to surrender all that he had to his enemy, how much more should we openly speak these words to our loving Heavenly Father willingly? (James 4:7a, 1 Peter 5:6, Mark 8:34) We have heard it before, but we need to hear it again very clearly: the condition of God's blessing is absolute surrender of all into His hands. Praise God! If our hearts are willing for that, there is no end to what God will do for us, in us, and through us; and there is no end to the blessing God will bestow.

Andrew Murray had often used the words, "absolute surrender" in his life. Then, one day he was with a group of Christians talking about the greatest need of believers and the church. A godly Christian with substantial experience in training workers for Christ answered the question of this greatest need quite simply. His response was, "Absolute surrender to God is the one thing." He continued, "If Christians are sound on this one point, they are willing to be taught and helped, and they always improve. On the other hand, those who are not sound on this one point most often leave the work. The condition for obtaining God's full blessing is absolute surrender to Him."

The words of this godly man struck Andrew Murray as never before, thus changing the course of his life forever. It is by God's grace that we desire to reiterate these truths Mr. Murray discovered and spent the rest of his life preaching about, and living out. The message is this: that your God in heaven answers the prayers which you have offered for blessing on yourselves and for blessing on those around you by this one demand - Are you willing to surrender yourselves absolutely into His hands? What will your answer be? God knows there are thousands of hearts who have said it. Also, there are thousands more who long to say it, but hardly dare to do so. Still, there are hearts who have said it, but who have failed miserably, and feel condemned because they did not find the secret of the power to live that life. May God have a word for each of us!

## God Expects Your Surrender

First of all, God claims absolute surrender from us. Yes, it has its foundation in the very nature of God. God cannot do otherwise. Who is God? He is the Fountain of life, the only Source of existence, power, and goodness. Throughout the universe there is nothing good but what God works. All of creation is absolutely surrendered to God. He has created the world and everything in it, including the sun, moon, stars, flowers, trees, and grass. Are they not all absolutely surrendered to God? Do they not allow God to work in them just what He pleases? Without surrender, there would be chaos in the working and no symmetry in God's universe. For example, when God clothes the lily with its beauty, is it not yielded up, surrendered, and given over to God as He works its beauty into it? Does this lily allow God to work in it just what He pleases? Do you think God can do His work in the lily if only half or a part of it is surrendered? He cannot. Likewise God's redeemed child, oh, do you think that God can do His work in you if there is only half or a part of you surrendered? God cannot do it. May we learn from creation to let God work His will in us by being completely surrendered! God is life, love, blessing, power, and infinite beauty. God delights in communicating to every child who is prepared to receive Him. But ah! This one lack of absolute surrender is just the thing that hinders God.

We all know in daily life what absolute surrender is. We know that everything has to be given up to its special, definite purpose and service. For example, think of the purpose of a pen. We know that if we use a pen in the way it was created to be used, it will be absolutely surrendered to the one work of writing. However, the pen must be absolutely surrendered to your hand if you are to write properly with it. If someone else holds it partly, you cannot write properly. In the same manner, your coat is absolutely given up to you to cover your body. Otherwise, it would only partially cover you. And now, do you expect that in your immortal being, in the divine nature that you have received by regeneration, God can work His work, every day and every hour, unless you are entirely given up to Him? God cannot. The temple of Solomon was absolutely surrendered to God when it was dedicated to Him. Every one of us is a temple of God, in which God will dwell and work mightily on one condition – absolute surrender to Him. God claims it, God is worth it, and without it God cannot work His blessed work in us. God not only claims it, but God will work it Himself, as we will see.

## Why is This Concept So Hard to Grasp?
## God Accomplishes Your Surrender

There are many hearts that say, "Ah, but absolute surrender implies so much!" One may say, "Oh, I have passed through so much trial and suffering, and there is so much of the self-life still remaining. I dare not face entirely surrendering because I know it will cause so much trouble and agony." God does not ask you to give the perfect surrender in your strength, or by the power of your will. God is willing to work it in you. Doesn't Philippians 2:13 assure us, "for it is God who works in you both to will and to do for His good pleasure?" May we go on our faces before God until our hearts believe that the everlasting God Himself will come in to turn out what is wrong! He will conquer what is evil, and work what is well pleasing in His blessed sight. God Himself will work it in you.

Look at the men in the Old Testament, such as Abraham. Do you think it was by accident that God found that man, the father of the faithful and the friend of God? Do you think that it was Abraham himself, apart from God, who had such faith, such obedience, and such devotion? You know it is not so. God raised him up and prepared him as an instrument for His glory. Also, did God not say to Pharaoh, "But indeed for this purpose I have raised you up, that I may show My power in you" (Exodus 9:16a)? And if God said that of him, will God not say it far more of every child of His?

Oh, may you be encouraged to cast away every fear! Come to Jesus with even a feeble desire. If there is the fear which says, "Oh, my desire is not strong enough. I am not willing for everything that may come, and I do not feel bold enough to say I can conquer everything." Know and trust your precious Lord and Savior afresh. Simply tell the Lord, "I am willing that You should make me willing." It is enough. If there is anything holding you back, or any sacrifice you are afraid of making, come to God now and prove how gracious your Jesus is. He will only command from you what He will bestow. It is not dependent upon you and your workings. God comes and offers to work this absolute surrender in you. All the searching, hungering, and longings in your heart are the drawings of the Divine Magnet, Jesus Christ. Jesus lived a life of absolute surrender. He has possession of you; He is living in your heart by His Holy Spirit. He desires to help you get ahold of Him entirely. He comes and draws you now by His message and words. Will you come and trust God to work in you this absolute surrender to Himself? Yes, blessed be God! He can do it, and He will do it. God not only claims it and works it, but God accepts it when we bring it to Him.

## God Accepts Your Surrender

God works in the quiet of our heart. God urges us by the hidden power of the Holy Spirit to come and speak it out; and we have to bring and yield to Him that absolute surrender. But remember, when you come and bring God that absolute surrender, it may, as far as your feelings or your consciousness go, be a thing of great imperfection. You may doubt, hesitate, and even say, "Is it absolute?" But, oh, remember there was once a man to whom Jesus said, "If you can believe, all things are possible to him who believes" (Mark 9:23). Still his heart was afraid, and he cried out, "Lord, I believe, help my unbelief" (Mark 9:24). That was a faith that triumphed over Satan, and the evil spirit was cast out. Come and say, "Lord, I yield myself in absolute surrender to You, my God." Even if you do so with a trembling heart and with the consciousness, "I do not feel the power. I do not feel the determination. I do not feel the assurance," it will succeed. Do not be afraid, but come - just as you are. Even in the midst of your trembling, the power of the Holy Spirit will work.

Have you not yet learned the lesson that the Holy Spirit works with mighty power, while on the human side everything appears feeble? Look at the Lord Jesus Christ in Gethsemane. We read that He, "through the eternal Spirit" (Hebrews 9:14), offered Himself as a sacrifice unto God. The Almighty Spirit of God was enabling Him to do it. Still, what agony, fear, and exceeding sorrow came over Him; and, oh, how He prayed! Externally, you can see no sign of the mighty power of the Spirit, but the Spirit of God was there. Likewise, while you are feeble, fighting, and trembling, have faith in the hidden work of God's Spirit, and do not fear. Trusting, yield yourself in spite of the fear.

When you do yield yourself in absolute surrender, let it be with the faith that God does now accept it. This is the great point and one that we often miss: that believers should be thus occupied with God in this matter of surrender. Be occupied with God. Be assured that God accepts your surrender regardless of your thoughts and feelings about it. We want to get help, every one of us, so that in our daily life God will be clearer to us, God will have the right place in our lives, and He will be "all in all" (I Corinthians 15:28). If we are going to have this throughout our lives,

5

let us begin now and look away from ourselves and look up to God. May each of us say, "I, a trembling child of God, with my failure, sin, and fear, bow before You. No one but You knows what passes through my heart. Oh, Lord, I accept Your terms. I have pleaded for blessings on myself and others. I have accepted Your terms of absolute surrender." While your heart says this to the Lord in deep silence, remember your God is present, taking note of it and writing it down in His book. You may not feel it or realize it, but God takes possession if you will trust Him. God not only claims and works your surrender, He also accepts it when you bring it, and He will maintain it.

## God Maintains Your Surrender

God maintains your surrender. This is a great difficulty with many. People say, "I have often been stirred at a meeting or a retreat, and I have consecrated myself to God. But it has passed away. I know it may last for a week or for a month, but it fades away. After a time it is all gone." This is because you do not believe that when God has begun the work of absolute surrender in you, and when God has accepted your surrender, then God holds Himself bound to care for it and keep it. Will you believe that? In this matter of surrender, there are two involved: God and you. The Lord is the everlasting and omnipotent Jehovah, and we are not. In the course of time as we come to know God, we grow to think more of Him and less of ourselves. When we finally believe and recognize His magnificence, holiness, and might, it makes it easier to trust ourselves to the will of our all-powerful God. Are you afraid to trust yourself to this mighty God now? God is able and willing. Do you believe that He can keep you continually, day by day, and moment by moment?

> "Moment by moment I'm kept in His love;
> Moment by moment I've life from above;
> Looking to Jesus till glory doth shine;
> Moment by moment, O Lord, I am Thine."[2]
> (Hymn by Daniel W. Whittle)

If God allows the sun to shine on you moment by moment without stopping, will God not let His life shine on you every moment? If you have not experienced it, it is because you have not trusted God for it, and you do not surrender yourself absolutely to God in that trust.

A life of absolute surrender has its difficulties. Yes, it has something far more than difficulties: it is a life that with men is absolutely impossible. But by the grace of God and the power of the Holy Spirit dwelling in us, it is a life to which we are destined, and a life that is possible for us! Praise God! Let us believe that God will maintain it.

George Muller, Christian evangelist and director of orphanages in Bristol, England during the 1800's, often told of God's goodness to him throughout his life. Mr. Muller attributed the secret of his happiness and all the blessing God had given him to two things. First, he had been enabled by grace to maintain a good conscience before God, day by day. The other was being a lover of God's Word. Ah, yes, a good conscience is achieved by aiming for complete obedience to God day by day. It is maintained through fellowship with God every day in His Word and in prayer. This is a life of absolute surrender.

Such a life has two sides. On one side, absolute surrender to do what God wants you to do. On the other side, to let God work what He wants to do.

First, to do what God wants you to do. Give yourself up absolutely to the will of God. We all know something of this will, but perhaps not enough of it. May we say absolutely to the Lord, "By Your grace I desire to do Your will in everything, every moment of the day. Help me, Lord God, that I have not a word upon my tongue but for Your glory; not a movement of my temper but for Your glory; not an affection of love or hate in my heart but for Your glory, and according to Your blessed will." God wants to bless you in a way beyond what you expect. From the beginning, "Eye has not seen, nor ear heard, nor have entered into the heart of man the things God has prepared for those who love Him" (1 Corinthians 2:9). God has prepared unheard of things – blessing more wonderful than you can imagine and more mighty than you can conceive. They are divine blessings. Oh, say now dear one, "I give myself absolutely to You God, to

7

Your will, and to do only what You want." It is God who will enable you to carry out the surrender.

On the other side, may we come to the Lord and say, "I give myself absolutely to You, Jesus, to let You work in me to will and do of Your good pleasure, as You have promised to do." The living God wants to work in His children in a way that we cannot understand, but that God's Word has revealed. He wants to work in us every moment of the day. God is willing to maintain our life. Let our absolute surrender be one of simple, childlike, and boundless trust.

## God Blesses When You Surrender

This absolute surrender to God brings wonderful blessings. What Ahab said to his enemy, King Ben-Hadad, "My lord, O king, just as you say, I and all that I have are yours," will we not say to our God and loving Father? If we do say it, God's blessing will come upon us. God wants us to be separate from the world (2 Corinthians 6:14-18). We are called to come out from the world that hates God. Come out for God and say, "Lord, anything for You." If you say that in prayer, God will accept it and He will teach you what it means.

Again, God will bless you. You have been praying for blessing. But do remember, there must be absolute surrender. At every tea table you see it. Why is tea poured into that cup? Because it is empty and given up for the tea! But put vinegar or coffee in your cup, will they pour the tea into the vessel? And can God fill you, can God bless you, if you are not absolutely surrendered to Him? He cannot. Let us believe God has wonderful blessings for us if we will but stand up for God and say, even with a trembling will, yet with a believing heart, "Oh God, I accept Your demands. I am Yours and all that I have. Absolute surrender is what my soul yields to You by divine grace."

You may not have such strong, clear feelings of surrender as you would like to have, but humble yourself in His sight, and acknowledge that you have grieved the Holy Spirit by your self-will, self-confidence, self-effort, and self-esteem. As you bow humbly before Him in the confession of this, just accept God's teaching that in our flesh dwells no good thing (Romans 7:18), and that nothing will help us except another life which must come in. We must deny self once and for all. Denying self must every moment be the power of your life. Then, Christ will come in and take possession. Peace is our harvest. It doesn't come when our flesh battles God for control. Are our hearts empty like the teacup, ready to be filled only with the Holy Spirit?

God, the Heavenly Father loves to give us the power of His Spirit. We have the Spirit of God dwelling within us. We come to God professing this, and praising God for it, and yet confessing how we have grieved the Spirit in areas where we are not yielded to Him. May we bow our knees to the Father and ask Him to strengthen us with all might by the Spirit in the inner man, and that He would fill us with His mighty power (Ephesians 3:14-21)! As the Spirit reveals Jesus to us, He will gladly fill our hearts with His grace, will, and power. Then, the self-life will be cast out. We cannot turn that around. First, we must yield to Him. Then, He will do the work through us.

Let us bow before God and confess with humility the state of the whole church. Think of the Christians around you - not people who live as nominal or professing Christians, but hundreds and thousands of honest Christians who are not living a life in the power of God or to His glory. They have so little power, so little devotion, and so little consecration to God. There is so little perception of the truth that a Christian is a person utterly surrendered to God's will! We are members of that sickly body. This sickliness of the body will hinder us and break us down unless we come humbly to God in confession, and separate ourselves from our partnership with worldliness and coldness toward each other. We must give ourselves up to be entirely and wholly for God.

How much Christian work is being done in the spirit of flesh and in the power of self! How much work is done, day by day, in human energy! Our will and our thoughts about the work are continually manifested with very little waiting upon God and upon the power of the Holy Spirit! Let us make a confession. In the church, and in our own lives, it is much easier to go with our feelings and our reasoning. We need to stop and listen to the Lord, so we can yield to Him. As we do this, His Holy Spirit will work in and through us.

Who truly longs to be delivered from the power of the self-life? Who truly acknowledges they are living in the power of self and the flesh? And, who is willing to cast all at the feet of Jesus? Beloved, there is deliverance. Do you love Jesus? Do you long to be in Jesus and be like Jesus? May a life full of fellowship with Jesus be to us the most desirable thing on earth! Do you think it is a hard thing to be called to be free from the world; and by that separation to be united to God and His love to live and walk with Him every day? Surely, one ought to say, "Anything to bring me to separation from the world, to live a life of full fellowship with God and Jesus."

Come and cast this self-life and flesh-life at the feet of Jesus. Then trust Him. Do not worry yourself with trying to understand it all. Instead, pray in faith that Jesus will come into your heart with the power of His resurrected life. Then, the Holy Spirit will bring His sanctifying power into your heart.

## Points to Ponder:

As A.W. Tozer was once noted to say, "If the Holy Spirit was withdrawn from the church today, 95 percent of what we do would go on, and no one would know the difference. If the Holy Spirit had been withdrawn from the New Testament church, 95 percent of what they did would stop, and everybody would know the difference."[3] Ponder this quote with the Lord. What are your thoughts on these statements? Do you see a correlation between the absolute surrender of the New Testament church and the blessings they received and bestowed on others? What about applying this quote to your own life?

# CHAPTER 2

## *The Fruit of The Spirit is Love*

"But the fruit of the Spirit is love, joy, peace, longsuffering,
kindness, goodness, faithfulness, gentleness, self-control.
Against such there is no law." Galatians 5:22-23

A LIFE FILLED WITH THE HOLY SPIRIT WILL REVEAL ITSELF IN OUR DAILY WALK
and conduct. In the Old Testament, God through the Holy Spirit
came upon people to reveal Himself and to give them the power to do
His work. But He did not dwell in them. Today, many people are content
with only this experience from the Lord. As New Testament Christians,
we submit to God in order that He works through us by the indwelling of
His Spirit, which will animate and renew our whole life. The Lord is not
only concerned about what we do, but who we are and how we live. If we
yield to the Spirit within, the outcome of our actions will be doing the
Lord's work, whatever He calls us to do. When God gives the Holy Spirit,
His great objective is the formation of holy character in us. It is a gift of a
holy mind and spiritual disposition. What we need above everything else
is to say, "I must have the Holy Spirit sanctifying my whole inner life if I
am really to live for God's glory."

When Jesus called His disciples, He called ordinary, imperfect men.
The difference between these men when first called by Christ and later
when they were filled with the Holy Spirit was truly miraculous. For
example, when the disciples James and John were frustrated with the
Samaritans, they went to Jesus. They asked if they could pull down fire

from heaven to destroy these people. (Luke 9:51-56) Where was the grace? Where was the love for others? They were full of the flesh. Even walking with Jesus daily for three years, witnessing His love, miracles, and grace toward others, didn't change their character. But, when they received the Holy Spirit, He equipped them as holy men for doing the work with power as Jesus intended it to be. Jesus spoke of power to the disciples, but it was the Spirit filling their whole being that worked the power.

Galatians 5:22 reads, "The fruit of the Spirit is love." Do we make it a daily habit to seek to be filled with the Holy Spirit as the Spirit of love? Has it been our experience that the more we are filled with the Holy Spirit, the more love we have for others? Undoubtedly, to the degree we allow ourselves to be filled with the Holy Spirit - that is the degree to which we can love others. It is no accident that the first fruit of the Spirit listed in Galatians 5:22 is love. When people accept the Holy Spirit into their lives, the first thing they usually notice is a new love in their hearts from God and a new love for others. This unconditional love that has flooded our hearts is given to us not only for us, but it is to be showered onto others in our lives. Oh, let us pray that God will help us get ahold of the simple, heavenly truth that if we are united in love for one another, Almighty God will do His blessed work among us - in our families, in our churches, in neighborhoods, in cities, and the world. Give yourselves up to love and the Holy Spirit will come; receive the Spirit, and He will teach you to love more. Won't you tell Him today, "I give myself up to You Lord, in order that through the power of your Holy Spirit I may love others with the love You give to me?"

## God is Love

Why is it that the fruit of the Spirit is love? It is because God is love (1 John 4:8). What does that mean? It is the very nature and being of God to delight in communicating Himself. God has no selfishness; God keeps nothing to Himself. God's nature is to be always giving. You see it in the sun, moon, and stars, in every flower, in every bird in the air, in every fish in the sea. God communicates life to His creatures. Also, where do the angels around

His throne, and the seraphim and cherubim who are flames of fire, get their glory? It comes from God because He is love, and He imparts to them His brightness and His blessedness. Likewise, God delights to pour His love into us, His redeemed children. Why? It is because God keeps nothing for Himself. From eternity God had His only begotten Son, and the Father gave Him all things. Nothing that God had was kept back. And, he has kept back nothing from us – even His only begotten Son. The Spirit of God is love and the fruit of the Spirit is love. When the Holy Spirit comes to us and to other men, will He be less a Spirit of love? It cannot be. He cannot change His nature.

## Mankind Needs Love

One great need of mankind is the thing which Christ's redemption came to accomplish: to restore love to this world. When man sinned, why was it that he sinned? Selfishness triumphed - he sought self instead of God. And just look! Adam at once begins to accuse the woman of having led him astray. Love for God had gone; love for each other was lost. Look again: of the first two children of Adam, one becomes a murderer of his brother. Doesn't this teach us that sin robbed the world of love? Even heathens can show love to one another, but it is only a little remnant of the love that was lost. One of the worst things sin did for man was to make him selfish, for selfishness cannot love. But don't despair! The answer is Jesus.

The Lord Jesus Christ came down from heaven as the Son of God's love. "God so loved the world that He gave His only begotten Son" (John 3:16). Jesus demonstrated what love is, and was an example to His disciples by living a life of love in fellowship with them. Jesus showed compassion to the poor and miserable, loved his enemies, and saved us because of His great love. Furthermore, when He went to heaven, He sent down the Spirit of Love to banish selfishness, envy, and pride, and to bring the love of God into the hearts of men. "The fruit of the Spirit is love." One of the last things Jesus said to His disciples was, "even as I have loved you, so you love one another" (John 13:34-35). Jesus' dying love was to be the only law of their conduct and fellowship with each other. What a message to

13

those fishermen, to those men full of pride and selfishness! By the grace of God, they were able to love one another as Jesus had loved them. When Pentecost came, they were of one heart and one soul. Jesus did it for them and in them.

Now, God calls us to live and walk in love. In order to be a testimony to Jesus, we must wear the badge of His love. Let's humbly ask Him for it. God is able to give it to us. "By this all will know that you are My disciples, if you have love for one another." John 13:35

## Love Conquers Selfishness

Why is the fruit of the Spirit love? It is because nothing but love can expel and conquer our selfishness. Self is a great curse, whether it's in relation to God, or to our fellow man, fellow Christians, or simply in seeking our own way. Our biggest challenge is not the lack of power to do God's work or for power to receive God's blessings, but for the power to have full deliverance from self. But, praise God, Jesus came to redeem us from self! By the power of Christ's love in us, we are able to experience deliverance from self-righteousness in fellowship with God, and unloving fellowship with each other. Deliverance from self-life means we are vessels overflowing with love in knowledge and all discernment (Philippians 1:9-10). This is why we pray for the power of the Holy Spirit for full deliverance from self. Deliverance is possible because the fruit of the Spirit is love. Jesus' glorious promise is that He is able to fill our hearts with love.

A great many of us try hard at times to love, but yet our love fails. The reason is simply this: because we have never learned to believe and accept the truth that the Holy Spirit can pour God's love into our hearts. The blessed words of Romans 5:5 which tell us, "the love of God is shed abroad in our hearts," has often been limited to mean the love of God to me. This is only the beginning. The love of God is always the love of God in its entirety, in its fullness as an indwelling power. It is the love of God to me which is reciprocated back to Him in love, and overflows to others in love. The three are one; you cannot separate them. Do believe that the love of God can be shed abroad in your heart and mind so that you can love all day long. How little we have understood or prayed for this love.

Why is the lamb always gentle? It is because that is its nature. Does it cost the lamb any trouble to be gentle? No. Why not? It is so beautiful and gentle. Does the lamb have to study to be gentle? No. Why does that come so easy to the lamb? The lambs' gentleness comes easy to it because gentleness is its nature. Look at a wolf. Why does it cost a wolf no trouble to be cruel to a poor lamb or sheep? It is because that is the wolf's nature. It does not have to summon up its courage for this. The wolf-nature is there.

Now, how can I have God's love for others? I cannot until the Spirit of God's love fills my heart and I begin to long for God's love in a very different sense from which I have sought it so selfishly: as a comfort, a joy, a happiness, and a pleasure for myself. I will never obtain this love until I realize that "God is love" and to claim it and receive it as an indwelling power for denying our selfish desires. I will never obtain it until I begin to see that my glory and my blessedness is to be like Jesus, in giving up everything in myself in absolute surrender to our Heavenly Father. May God work this in us! Oh, the divine blessedness of the love with which the Holy Spirit can fill our hearts! The fruit of the Spirit is love. Continually pray for the power to be fully delivered from self and to have this love for others.

## Love is God's Gift

How do we know if we are truly filled with God's love? For many of us, our temper is an indicator of where we really are with God. Just as the hands of a clock reveal what is going on within the clock, our tempers reveal what is going on within our hearts. If I see the hands stand still or point wrong or the clock is slow or fast, I know that the clock is not working properly. Temper is a proof of whether the love of Christ is filling our hearts or not. Sometimes it seems to be easier to show love to others outside our homes than to our own family. Where is the love of God? It is in Jesus. God has prepared for us a wonderful redemption in Jesus, and He longs to make something supernatural of us. He longs to conform us to His image, which always loves. Do we long for it, ask for it, and expect it in its fullness?

Then there is the issue of our tongue. "Let your speech always be with grace, seasoned with salt" (Colossians 4:6a). When we speak, love should always be our motivation. When we speak about others, how often there are sharp remarks! May we all say, "Lord Jesus, 'Keep me from saying anything that would be unloving! Shut my mouth if I am not going to speak in tender, truthful love (Ephesians 4:15)'" Sadly, how often sharp criticism, sharp judgement, hasty opinion, unloving words, secret contempt of each other, or sacred condemnation of each other are found among Christians who are banded together in work! Beloved, think of how a mother loves her children. A mother's love blankets her children, and she delights in them with the tenderest of compassion, even with their shortcomings or failures. In like manner, there ought to be in the heart of every believer a motherly love toward every brother or sister in Christ. Have you aimed at that? Have you sought it? Have you ever pleaded for it? Jesus Christ said, "A new commandment I give to you, that you love one another; as I have loved you, that you also love one another" (John 13:34). If the Lord has filled our hearts with the love of His Holy Spirit, our speech should reflect this.

It is in our daily life and conduct that the fruit of the Spirit is love. From that come all the graces and virtues in which love is manifested: joy, peace, longsuffering, gentleness, goodness, kindness, and meekness. There is to be no sharpness or hardness in our tone, no unkindness or selfishness, and meekness before God and man. You notice that these are the gentler virtues. Colossians 3:12 instructs us, "Therefore, as the elect of God, holy and beloved, put on tender mercies, kindness, humility, meekness, longsuffering." All of these tender virtues are closely connected with our dependence on the Holy Spirit. They are indeed heavenly graces. Jesus needed to come from heaven to teach us that our blessedness is longsuffering, meekness, and kindness and our glory is humility before God. The fruit of the Spirit that He brought from heaven out of the heart of the crucified Jesus, and that He gives in our heart, is first and foremost, love.

We speak of grieving the Holy Spirit by worldliness, ritualism, formality, error, and indifference, but what about our lack of love for our brothers and sisters in Christ? May every heart search itself, and ask that God may search it. Why are we taught that 'the fruit of the Spirit is love?' It is because the Spirit of God has come to make our daily life an exhibition of divine power, and a revelation of what God can do for His children.

## Our Love Shows God's Power

In the second and fourth chapters of Acts, we read that the disciples were of one heart and of one soul. During the three years they had walked with Jesus, they never had been in that spirit. All of Jesus' teachings and His example could not make them be of one heart and one soul. But, when the Holy Spirit came from heaven, He shed the love of God into their hearts and they were of one heart and one soul. The same Holy Spirit that brought the love of Heaven into their hearts must fill us, too. Nothing less will do. No amount of Bible studies, or church attendance, or Christian service will cause us to know the true love of Christ. Just as Jesus did, one might preach love for three years with the tongue of an angel, but that would not teach any man to love unless the power of the Holy Spirit brought the love of heaven into his heart.

If we want to pray in power, and if we want to expect the Holy Spirit to come down in power, and if we indeed want God to pour out His Spirit, we must enter into a covenant with God that we will love one another with a heavenly love. Just as it was for the disciples, we too must be filled with the Holy Spirit in order to truly love. Are you ready for that? Only true love is large enough to take in all God's children. If my vow of absolute surrender to God was sincere, then it must mean being open for the Divine Love to fill me. I must be a servant of love in order to love every child of God around me according to knowledge and all discernment, for the fruit of the Spirit is love (Philippians 1:9-11). Forgive us, Lord, for degrading the Holy Spirit into a mere power by which we have to do our work! Oh, that the Holy Spirit might be held in honor as a power to fill us with the very life and nature of God and of Christ!

## Christian Work Requires Love

"The fruit of the Spirit is love." Once again, why is this so? It is because love is the only power in which Christians really can do their work. Yes, it is love that we need. We want not only love that is to bind us to each other, but we want a divine love in our work for the lost around us. Do we not often take on a great deal of work from a natural spirit of compassion for people, or because our pastor or friend calls us to it? It must be God's love in our heart calling us to the task. Nothing else will suffice. We cannot fulfill every need around us, but we can fulfill the needs Jesus calls us to, yet only by His love flowing through us and only at His command. May we all plead, "Lord, let love from heaven flow down into my heart! May I pray and live like one who is overflowing with Your everlasting love dwelling in my heart! Let it be a continual filling for pouring out onto others."

Ah, yes, if the love of God were in our hearts, what a difference it would make! There are hundreds of believers who say, "I work for Jesus, and I feel I could work much harder, but I do not have the gift. I do not know how or where to begin. I do not know what I can do." Beloved brethren, ask God to baptize you with the Spirit of love, and love will find its way. Love is a fire that will burn through every difficulty. You may be a shy, hesitating person who cannot speak well, but love can burn through everything. God fills us with love! We need it for our work. You have heard many touching stories of love expressed, and you have responded, "How beautiful." Here is one such story:

There was once a lady who had been asked to speak at a rescue home for poor women. As she arrived there and passed by the window with the host, she saw a wretched woman sitting outside, and asked,

"Who is that?"

The host replied, "She has been into the house 30 or 40 times, but has always gone away again. Nothing can be done with her. She is so low and hard."

But the lady insisted, "She must come in."

The host responded, "We have been waiting for you. Everyone has gathered and you have only an hour for your speech."

The lady replied, "No. This is more important," and she went outside where the woman was sitting.

She asked, "What is the matter, my sister?"

"I am not your sister," was the reply.

The lady laid her hand on her shoulder, and said, "Yes, I am your sister, and I love you." She continued thus speaking until the heart of the poor woman was touched.

The conversation lasted some time, and the other women were patiently waiting inside. Ultimately, the lady brought the woman into the room. There was the poor, wretched, degraded woman, full of shame. She would not sit on a chair with the others, but sat down on a stool beside the speaker. The speaker let the woman lean against her, and she wrapped her arms lovingly around the poor woman while she spoke to the assembled people. That love touched the woman's heart, for she had found one who really loved her. It was this love which made a way for the love of Jesus to enter her heart.

Praise God for there is love on earth in the hearts of God's children! Let there be more, sweet Jesus! Oh, that God would begin with us now, and grant each of us this tender heavenly love for others!

## Love Inspires Intercession

Once again, only the love of Jesus can fit us for the work of intercessory prayer. We have seen that love must fit us for our work. The hardest and most important work to be done for our sinful world is the work of intercession - going to God and taking time to lay hold of Him. A man may be an earnest Christian and do many good things, but how often must he confess that he knows little of what it is to tarry with God. May God give us the great gift of an intercessory spirit – a spirit of prayer and supplication! May we all in the name of Jesus not let a day pass without praying for all Christians!

It seems there are Christians who think little of that. We have prayer meetings where we pray for our members, but not for all believers everywhere. May we take time to pray for God's church and His people! It is right to pray for the heathen. God help us to pray more for them. It is right to pray for missionaries, for evangelistic work, and for the unconverted. Additionally, in Ephesians 6:18, Paul instructs us to pray for believers. Let's make this our first prayer every day, "Lord, bless Christians everywhere." Plead for God to visit His people, plead for each other, and plead for all believers who are trying to work for God. Let love fill your heart. Ask Jesus to pour fresh love into you every day. Try to grasp, by the Holy Spirit of God: I am separated unto the Holy Spirit, and the fruit of the Spirit is love. God help us to understand it.

May God grant that we learn day by day to wait more quietly upon Him. We must not wait upon God only for ourselves, or the power to do so will soon be lost. Instead, we must give ourselves up to the ministry and the love of intercession - to pray more for God's people in general, for God's people around us, for the Spirit of love in ourselves and in them, and for the work of God we are connected with. The answer will surely come, and our waiting upon God will be a source of untold blessing and power. "The fruit of the Spirit is love."

Do you have a lack of love to confess before God? Then make your confession and say before Him, "Oh Gracious Lord, my lack of heart, my lack of love, I confess it. Begin with me now, and fill me with your heavenly love!" Then, as you cast your confession at His feet, believe that Jesus cleanses you, that Jesus comes in His mighty, cleansing, saving power to deliver you, and that He will give His Holy Spirit to you. "The fruit of the Spirit is love."

## Points to Ponder:

This chapter examined the fact that a lamb is always gentle because its nature is gentle. The Holy Spirit's nature is to always love. Our self-nature is to always be selfish. Whose nature do you emulate most often? This is a very hard question to answer honestly, but in all truthfulness, without surrendering to the Holy Spirit, our nature exhibits selfishness. You can believe that the love of God can be shed abroad in your heart and mind (Romans 5:5). Will you join us in praying this scripture over our lives today? Jesus loves everyone, but He interacted with the religious leaders differently than he did with His disciples. Our love must be according to knowledge and all discernment so that we approve of the things which are excellent (Philippians 1:9-11).

**IMPORTANT:** This chapter discussed in detail that we are commissioned by God to love others. However, this does NOT mean God wants you to stay in any kind of abusive situation. If you are living in any kind of abuse, we plead with you to get help from others. Your safety and well-being is of utmost importance! Seek God's wisdom and guidance in prayer to help you find a trustworthy person in which to confide. It could be a friend, family member, pastor, counselor at church, or even a domestic abuse organization. (The National Domestic Abuse Hotline number is 800-799-7233.)

# CHAPTER 3

## *Separated Unto The Holy Spirit*

"Now in the church that was at Antioch there were certain prophets and teachers: Barnabas, Simeon who was called Niger, Lucius of Cyrene, Manaen who had been brought up with Herod the tetrarch, and Saul. As they ministered to the Lord and fasted, the Holy Spirit said, 'Now separate to Me Barnabas and Saul for the work to which I have called them.' Then, having fasted and prayed, and laid hands on them, they sent them away. So, being sent out by the Holy Spirit, they went down to Seleucia, and from there they sailed to Cyprus." Acts 13:1-4

IN THE STORY OF OUR TEXT, WE FIND SOME PRECIOUS THOUGHTS TO GUIDE US TO what God would have of us, and what God would do for us. The great lesson of the verses quoted is this: The Holy Spirit is the director of God's work here on earth. And what we should do if we are to rightly work for God, and if God is to bless our work, is to see that we stand in a right relationship with the Holy Spirit. We must see that we give Him the place of honor that belongs to Him every day. In all our work and (what is more) in all our private, inner life, the Holy Spirit must always have the first place. Let's look at some of the precious thoughts this passage suggests.

## God's Plans

First, God has His own plans in regard to His Kingdom. Regardless of Paul and Barnabas' plans, God had certain plans and intentions with regard to Asia and Europe. He had conceived them, they were His, and He made them known to His servants.

As a commander has orders and plans for the movement of his troops and the architect has plans for the building, so does the Lord have plans for each of our lives. When we came to Christ, we entered a new reality. No longer would the things of this world be our top priority. No longer would we be directed by feelings, emotions, and our own dreams. We have entered a realm with the King of the universe who sees all things and knows all things. We are now to be aware of the gifts He has given us through His Holy Spirit, and are to be ready to use them wherever He directs.

Jesus told his disciples that they were not to worry about the mundane things of life, like what they should eat and what to wear. He also gave the examples of the birds being fed and the flowers being clothed by God. Of course we live in this physical world, so we have to eat and certainly we have to cloth our body, but these are needs our Heavenly Father will see after. Our mind and heart now should be focused on the calling of the Lord each and every day. As we do this, through quiet time in prayer and Bible reading, we are connecting with our Commander in Chief. Here, God impresses on our heart His purpose for each day, and He will direct us in all instances. We simply have to be faithful in our obedience to carry out what He puts before us.

Our great Commander will organize every campaign. His generals and officers do not always know the great plans. They often receive sealed orders, and they have to wait for Him to reveal their contents. God in heaven has a plan and a will in regard to any work that ought to be done, and to the way in which it has to be done. Blessed is the man who receives God's secrets and works under Him.

Let's think of constructing a new building in a large city. When the work begins, demolition of the old building is done first. Nothing but trash, broken concrete, bricks, and ruins from the old building can be seen. After the rubble is cleared, a foundation is laid, and very few know what the building will be that will rise. No one knows it perfectly in every detail except one man, the architect. In his mind, it is all clear, and as the contractors, masons, and carpenters come to do their work, they take their orders from him. The humblest laborer has to be obedient to the orders. Then, the structure will rise and a beautiful building will be completed. And just so, when we walk each day in the guidance of the Holy Spirit, we are laying the foundation of a work in which only God knows what it is to become.

God has His workers and His plans clearly mapped out. Our position is to wait so that God may communicate to us as much of His will as is needful. We simply have to be faithful in our obedience, carrying out His orders. God has a plan for His people and His church on earth. However, we too often make our own plan. We think that we know what ought to be done. We ask God to bless our feeble fleshly efforts, instead of absolutely refusing to go unless God goes before us. God has planned for the work and the extension of His Kingdom. The Holy Spirit has had that work given in charge to Him: "The work to which I have called them" (Acts 13:2). May God, therefore, help us all to be afraid of "touching the ark of God" (2 Samuel 6:6), except as we are led by the Holy Spirit.

## God's Will Revealed

Secondly, God is willing and able to reveal His will to His servants. Praise God that communications still come down from heaven! As we read in the Acts passage what the Holy Spirit said, so the Spirit will still speak to His church and His people. In these latter days, He has often done it. He has come to individual men, and by His divine teaching He has led them out into fields of labor that others could not at first understand or approve. He has led them into ways and methods that did not appeal to the majority. But the Holy Spirit still, in our time, teaches His people. Thank God, in our foreign missions, in our home, and in a thousand forms of work, the guiding of the Holy Spirit is known. But, may we all confess, He is too little known. We have not learned to wait upon Him enough, and so we should make this solemn declaration before God: "Oh God, we want to wait more for You to show us Your will."

Do not ask God only for power. Many Christians have their own plan of working and their own will, but ask God for the power. Often this is why God gives so little grace, power, and success. It is both God's will and His power that are needed. Let us take our place before God, and say, "What is done in the will of God, the strength of God will not be withheld from it. What is done in the will of God must have the mighty blessing of God." So, let our first desire be to have the will of God revealed.

Some may ask if it is easy to get these communications from God and to understand them. It is easy for those who are in right fellowship with heaven, and who understand the art of waiting on God in prayer. How often people ask, "How can a person know the will of God?" And people want, when they are in perplexities or difficulties, to pray very earnestly so that God will answer them at once. But God can only reveal His will to a heart that is humble, tender, and empty. God can only reveal His will in perplexities and special difficulties to a heart that has learned to obey and honor Him loyally in little things and in daily life.

## Our Disposition

Thirdly, note the disposition to which the Spirit revealed God's will to these men in the Acts passage. There were a number of men ministering to the Lord, serving Him with prayer and fasting. What a deep conviction they have! It is as if they are saying, "It must all come directly from heaven. We are in fellowship with the risen Lord. We must have a close union with Him, and somehow He will let us know what He wants." And there they were empty, willing, helpless, glad, joyful, and deeply humbled. They, as Jesus' servants, were seemingly waiting upon the Lord to reveal His will in fasting and prayer. And the Holy Spirit came and spoke to them.

Peter is another example of a person who sincerely wanted to know God's will. He was on the housetop fasting and praying when the Lord gave him the same vision three times. As you know, the Jewish people at that time were restricted from eating the foods God was commanding Peter to eat in the vision. All of this was to prepare Peter to go to Caesarea to the home of Cornelius, who was a God-fearing Roman centurion. Until that time, Peter was reluctant to preach the gospel to anyone except the Jews. The Lord sent three men to bring Peter to Cornelius' home to proclaim the Gospel. As the Lord had ordained, all who listened to Peter were saved. This was not in Peter's plans, but because he desired to fulfill God's will, the Lord used him to bring unlikely people to Himself.

It is in hearts entirely surrendered to the Lord Jesus, separating themselves from the world (even from ordinary religious exercises), and giving themselves up in intense prayer to look to their Lord, that the heavenly will of God will be made manifest.

Notice that the word "fasted" occurs twice in our passage in Acts. "They fasted and prayed." When we pray, we love to go into our closet, according to the command of Jesus, and shut the door. We shut out business, company, pleasure, and anything that can distract because we want to be alone with God. But in one way, even the material world follows us there. We must eat. In the Acts passage, these men wanted to shut themselves out from the influences of the material and the visible, and they fasted. What they ate was simply enough to supply the wants of nature. In the intensity of their souls, they thought to give expression to their letting go of everything on earth in their fasting before God. Oh, may God give us that intensity of desire – that separation from everything – because we want to wait upon God, so that the Holy Spirit may reveal to us God's blessed will!

## God's Will: Separation unto the Holy Spirit

Fourthly, what is the will of God as the Holy Spirit reveals it? It is contained in one phrase: Separation unto the Holy Spirit. That is the keynote of the message from heaven. "Separate to me Barnabas and Saul for the work to which I have called them. The work is Mine, and I care for it. I have chosen these men and called them. I want you who represent Jesus' church upon earth to set them apart unto Me."

Look at this heavenly message in its twofold aspect. The men were to be set apart to the Holy Spirit, and the Church was to do this separating work. The Holy Spirit could trust these men to do it in a right spirit. There they were abiding in fellowship with the Holy Spirit. These were the men the Holy Spirit had prepared, and He could say of them, "Let them be separated to me."

Here we come to the very root – the very life of the need of every Christian worker. The question is: What is needed so that the power of God would rest on me more mightily? What is needed so that the blessing of God would be poured out more abundantly among those perishing sinners among whom we labor? The answer from heaven is: "I want men and women separated unto the Holy Spirit."

What does "being separated upon the Holy Spirit" imply? When Jesus spoke about the Holy Spirit, he said, "The world cannot receive Him" (John 14:17). Paul said, "We have received not the spirit of the world, but the Spirit that is of God" (1 Corinthians 2:12). This is the great need in every Christian worker - the spirit of the world going out and the Spirit of God coming in to take possession of the inner life and the whole being.

We should not be satisfied with the Holy Spirit just giving us power for work. When we feel a measure of the power of the Holy Spirit, and receive blessing, we thank God for it. But, God wants something more and something higher for us. God wants us to seek the Holy Spirit as a Spirit of power in our own heart and life in order to conquer self, cast out sin, and be conformed into the blessed and beautiful image of Jesus. If we limit the power of the Holy Spirit in our lives, we may be saved, but we will not be used to help people grow to a higher standard of spiritual life.

But a man who is separated unto the Holy Spirit is a man who is given up to say, "Father, let the Holy Spirit have full dominion over me - in my home, in my temper, in every word of my tongue, in every thought of my heart, in every feeling toward my fellow-men. Let the Holy Spirit have entire possession." Is that what has been the longing and the covenant of your heart with your God – to be a man or a woman separated and given up unto the Holy Spirit? May you heed the voice of heaven calling, "Separate yourself unto the Holy Spirit!" May God grant that the Word may enter into the very depths of our being to search us, and if we discover that we have not come out from the world entirely – if God discloses to us that self-life, self-will, or self-exaltation are there – let us humble ourselves before Him and cry out, "Separate me unto the Holy Spirit."

Man, woman, brother, sister, you are a worker separated unto the Holy Spirit. Is that true? Has that been your longing desire? Has that been your surrender? Has that been what you have expected through faith in the power of our Risen and Almighty Lord Jesus? If not, here is the call of faith, and here is the key to blessing – separated unto the Holy Spirit. God write the words in our hearts!

As for the church that was to do the separating of these men, the Holy Spirit spoke to that church as a church capable of doing that work. The Holy Spirit trusted them. God grant that our churches, our missionary societies, plus all our directors, councils, and committees may be comprised of men and women who are fit for the work of separating workers unto the Holy Spirit. We ask You, God, for that, too.

## Consciousness and Action

Lastly, this holy partnership with the Holy Spirit in this work becomes a matter of consciousness and of action. What did these men do? They set apart Paul and Barnabas. Then, it is written of the two that they, being sent forth by the Holy Spirit, went down to Seleucia. Oh, what fellowship! The Holy Spirit was doing His part of the work, while the men were doing their part. After the ordination of the men on earth, it is written in God's inspired Word that they were sent forth by the Holy Spirit.

Beloved, do you see how this partnership calls to new prayer and fasting? They had for a certain time been ministering to the Lord and fasting. Then, the Holy Spirit speaks and they have to do the work, and to enter into partnership. At once, they come together for more prayer and fasting. That is the spirit in which they obey the command of their Lord. This teaches us that it is not only the beginning of our Christian work, but all along, that we need to have our strength in prayer. May we accept and grasp our need for prayer. The wonderful power that prayer is meant to have in our lives is often not utilized! Lord Jesus, by Your grace, in prayer teach us new things. Forgive us, Lord for we have so little availed ourselves of prayer.

What a wonderful blessing comes when the Holy Spirit is allowed to lead, empower, and direct the work, and when it is carried out in obedience to Him! The Holy Spirit has been called, "the executive of the Holy Trinity." He has not only power, but He has the Spirit of love. Since He is willing to bless every sphere of this dark world, why is there not more blessing? The only feasible answer can be that we, as Christians, have not honored Him as we should. Is not every thoughtful heart ready to cry, "God, forgive me that I have not honored the Holy Spirit as I should have. I have grieved Him in that I have allowed self, flesh, and my own will to actually have the place that You wanted the Holy Spirit to have." Herein is a reason there is so much division, feebleness, and failure in the body of Christ today.

## Points to Ponder:

In our walk with the Lord, we need to continue with the same zeal that we had at the beginning. It is so easy to forget the necessity of yielding to the Holy Spirit. We can so easily get into habits – which are flesh, instead of depending solely on the Holy Spirit. This is where Paul gives the warning in the third chapter of Galatians, "having begun in the Spirit, are you now made perfect by the flesh?" This is a powerful warning from our Lord of the danger we can get into when walking in the flesh. We may not even recognize it, but eventually our spirits will become dry. We will lose the joy of knowing Jesus and walking in His power anew each day. This is where the walk in the Spirit becomes a walk in religion. Let's spend some time in prayer asking the Lord to search our hearts and to separate us again unto the Holy Spirit to accomplish His purposes in and through us.

# CHAPTER 4

## *God's Call to Bring Us to the End of Ourselves*

"And the Lord turned and looked at Peter. Then Peter remembered the word of the Lord, how He had said to him, 'Before the rooster crows, you will deny Me three times.' So Peter went out and wept bitterly." Luke 22:61-62

THAT WAS THE TURNING POINT IN THE LIFE OF PETER. JESUS HAD SAID TO HIM, "You cannot follow me now" (John 13:36). Peter was not in a state fit to follow Christ, because he had not been brought to the end of himself. He did not know himself, and he therefore could not follow Jesus. But, when he went out and wept bitterly, then came the great change. This was the turning point in Peter's life. Jesus had told Peter that when he was converted, he was to strengthen his brothers (Luke 22:32). He didn't understand that yet, but soon he will, and soon he does. He needed to be converted from self to Christ and that day was here. Peter's repentance gives us all hope for our walk with the Lord; he is a picture of a changed heart and a new person in Christ.

Thank God for the story of Peter. He is a man in the Bible who gives great comfort to Christians. When we look at his character, so full of failures, and at what Christ made him by the power of the Holy Spirit, there is hope for every one of us. But remember, before Christ could fill Peter with the Holy Spirit and make a new man of him, he had to go out and weep bitterly - he had to be humbled. To help understand this transformation, let's look at four points in Peter's life. First, let us look at

Peter, the devoted disciple of Jesus; next, at Peter as he lived the life of self; then, at Peter in his repentance; and last, at what Jesus made of Peter by the Holy Spirit.

## Peter - the Devoted Disciple of Jesus

First and foremost, Peter was a devoted disciple of Jesus Christ. Jesus called Peter to forsake his nets and follow Him (Matthew 4:18-20). Peter did it at once, and afterward he could correctly say to the Lord, "We have left all and followed You" (Matthew 19:27). Peter was a man of absolute surrender to Jesus. He gave up all to follow Jesus. Peter was also a man of ready obedience. You remember Jesus said to him, "Launch out into the deep and let down your nets for a catch." Peter the fisherman knew there were no fish there, for they had been fishing all night and had caught nothing. Nevertheless, he said, "At Your word I will let down the net" (Luke 5:4-5). He submitted to the word of Jesus. Furthermore, he was a man of great faith. When he saw Jesus walking on the sea, he asked the Lord to allow him to walk on the water (Matthew 14:28). At the voice of Jesus, in full faith he stepped out of the boat and walked on the water.

Also, Peter was a man of spiritual insight. When Jesus asked the disciples, "Who do you say that I am?" Peter was able to answer, "You are the Christ, the Son of the Living God." Jesus replied, "Blessed are you, Simon Bar-Jonah; for flesh and blood has not revealed that to you, but my Father who is in heaven" (Matthew 16:15-17). Jesus also spoke of Peter as the rock, and told him, "I will give you the keys of the kingdom of heaven" (Matthew 16:18-19). Although he displayed these incredible attributes of a strong believer in Christ, there was much self-life still in Peter.

## Peter Living the Life of Self

Soon after Jesus had said to Peter, "Flesh and blood has not revealed that to you, but my Father who is in heaven," Jesus began to speak about his sufferings. Peter dared to say, "Far be it from You, Lord; this shall not happen to You!" But Jesus turned and said to Peter, "Get behind Me,

Satan! You are an offense to Me, for you are not mindful of the things of God, but the things of men" (Matthew 16:22-23). This is great evidence of Peter's self-will and trusting his own wisdom by actually forbidding Jesus to go to the cross. By this statement, we know that Peter was still trusting in himself and his own thoughts about divine things. Peter wasn't unique in his thoughts of grandeur. All the disciples, at one time or another, questioned who should be the greatest and who had the right to the very first place. Each one sought his own honor above the others. The self-life was strong in them. The disciples left their old lives, but not their old selves.

When Jesus had spoken to Peter about His sufferings, and said "Get behind Me, Satan," He followed it up by saying, "If anyone desires to come after Me, let him deny himself, and take up his cross, and follow Me" (Matthew 16:24). No man can follow Jesus unless he does that. Self must be utterly denied. What does this mean? It is not self-denial, which involves taking something away from ourselves that we may want. Jesus is talking about denying our will in order to obey Him. We all know from our own life experience or from watching others, that before we can really understand what absolute surrender is about, we have to relinquish any ideas of what God should do in our lives. Peter's biggest fault was that he truly believed he had God's plans all figured out, as well as his place in these plans. Jesus told Peter that he must deny himself – that is, self must be ignored, and it's every claim or reasoning rejected. This is the root of true discipleship. But Peter did not understand it and could not obey it. Peter boasted to Jesus with self-confidence that even if all were made to stumble, he wouldn't stumble (Mark 14:27-31). He also declared that he was ready to go with Jesus to prison and to death (Luke 22:33). Peter was sincere and honest when he made his promises to Jesus, and he really intended to do it. Here we see an example of the flesh's best intentions and the impossibility of its performance. Peter was an amazing man, but he did not know himself. He did not believe that he was as bad as Jesus said he was – that he would actually deny Jesus three times! Yes, instead of denying self, Peter denied Jesus.

We perhaps think of individual sins that come between us and God. What are we to do with that self-life which is unclean and is our very nature? What are we to do with that flesh that is entirely under the power of sin? Deliverance from that is what we need. Peter did not have that deliverance. Therefore, it was in self-confidence that he went forth and denied his Lord.

Notice how Jesus uses the word "deny" twice. He first used the word when He told his disciples (including Peter), "Deny yourself" in Matthew 16:24. Jesus said to Peter the second time, "You will deny Me" in Matthew 26:34. It is either of the two. There is no other choice for us: we must either deny self or deny Jesus. If we don't deny self, we will deny Jesus. We are in a battle as the Scriptures reveal. There are two great powers fighting each other: the self-life in the power of sin and Jesus in the power of God. Either of these must rule within us.

It was self that made the devil. He was an angel of God, but wanted to exalt himself. Self was the cause of the fall of man. Eve wanted something for herself, and so our first parents fell into all the wretchedness of sin. We, their children, have inherited an awful nature of sin.

## Peter's Repentance

Peter denied his Lord three times, and then the Lord looked at him. That look of Jesus' broke Peter's heart. The terrible sin that he had committed, the terrible failure that had come, and the depth into which he had fallen, suddenly opened up before him. Can you imagine the shame, heartbreak, and hopeless despair Peter must have felt? Then, "Peter went out and wept bitterly." Oh, who can tell what that repentance must have been? During the following hours of that night, and the next day when he saw Jesus crucified and buried, what hopeless despair and shame he must have felt! His Lord was gone, his hope was gone, and he had denied his Lord. After that life of love and that blessed fellowship of three years with Jesus, Peter had denied his blessed Jesus. It's hard to imagine how hopeless he must have felt. However, this depth of sorrow and humiliation was the turning point for Peter. He was truly repentant.

After His resurrection, Jesus reminded Peter of his denial, by asking Peter if he loved him, three times. Peter replied, "Lord, You know all things; You know that I love You" (John 21:17). The Lord was affirming His love for Peter and releasing him from his guilt and shame. He was forgiven.

## Peter Transformed

Now Peter was prepared for deliverance from self. Jesus took Peter and the others to the footstool of the throne and told them to wait in Jerusalem (Luke 24:49-53). Then, on the day of Pentecost, the Holy Spirit came and Peter was a changed man. In Peter there was now such boldness, such power, such insight into the Scriptures, and such blessing with which he preached that day. Praise God for that! But there was something deeper and better which happened to Peter. His whole nature was changed. The work that Jesus began when He looked at him was perfected when he was filled with the Holy Spirit.

This change in Peter is evident in the book of 1 Peter. When Peter said to Jesus in effect, "You can never suffer - it cannot be," it shows he did not have a conception of what it was to pass through death into life. Also, when Jesus warned Peter, "You will deny me" (Matthew 26:34), and he insisted he never would, Peter showed how little he understood what was in himself. But, when we hear Peter say in 1 Peter 4:14a, "If you are reproached for the name of Christ, blessed are you, for the Spirit of glory and of God rests upon you," we see that it is not the old Peter. It is the very Spirit of Christ Jesus breathing and speaking within him.

Additionally, Peter tells us in 1 Peter 2:21, that we are called to suffer because Christ also suffered. We can see what a change had come over Peter. Instead of denying Jesus, Peter found joy and pleasure in denying himself. In Acts 5:29 when he was called before the Council, Peter could boldly say, "We ought to obey God rather than men," and return with the other disciples rejoicing that they were counted worthy to suffer shame for Jesus' name (Acts 5:41). You remember Peter's self-exaltation, but now he has found out that "the incorruptible beauty of a gentle and quiet spirit... is very precious in the sight of God" (1 Peter 3:4). Again in 1 Peter 5:5, he tells us to be submissive to one another, and be clothed with humility. Dear friend, look at Peter utterly changed. The self-pleasing, self-trusting, and self-seeking Peter is now filled with the Holy Spirit and the life of Jesus. Christ had done it for him by the Holy Spirit.

## The Point

Now, what is the point of this brief summary of Peter's life? This story is part of the history of every believer who is really to be made a blessing by God. This story reveals what everyone can receive from God. Let's glance at what these lessons teach us.

First, you may be a true believer who loves the Lord with all your heart, but you may still be living much of the self-life. This is a very solemn truth. Peter, before he denied Jesus, had cast out demons and had healed the sick. Yet, the flesh had power; and the flesh had room in him. Oh beloved, we have to realize that it is because there is so much of the self-life in us that the power of God cannot work in us as mightily as He desires that it should work. Do you realize that our great God is longing to double His blessing, to give tenfold blessing through us? But there is something hindering Him. It is the self-life. When we think of Peter's pride, impulsiveness, and self-confidence, it is all rooted in one word: self. Jesus had said, "Deny self," but Peter had never understood, and never obeyed. Every failing came out of that.

What a solemn thought, and what an urgent plea for us to cry, "Oh God, do show this to us so that none of us may be living the self-life." It has happened to people who have been Christians for years. It has happened to people who have perhaps occupied prominent positions. God found them out and taught them to find out about themselves. They became utterly ashamed and fell broken before God. Oh, the bitter shame, sorrow, pain, and agony that came to them, until at last they found out there was deliverance. Peter went out and wept bitterly. There may be many godly people in whom the power of the flesh still rules.

Secondly, it is the work of our blessed Lord Jesus to disclose the power of self. How was it that Peter - the carnal, self-willed, self-loved Peter - ever became a man of Pentecost and the writer of his epistles? It was because Jesus placed him in charge, Jesus watched over him, and Jesus taught and blessed him. The warnings that Jesus had given him were part of the training. Last of all, there came that look of love. In His suffering, Jesus did not forget Peter, but turned around and looked upon him. And the Christ who led Peter to Pentecost is waiting today to take charge of every heart that is willing to surrender to Him. Are there not some saying, "If I am honest with myself, my concern with self-life, self-comfort, self-consciousness, self-pleasing, and self-will happen more often than I want to admit. How can I get rid of it?" It is Jesus Christ who can rid you of it. No one else but Jesus Christ can give deliverance from the power of self. And what does He ask you to do? He asks that you humble yourself before Him.

**Points to Ponder:**

We can all relate to boasting in our flesh as Peter did, especially in the beginning of our Christian walk. We had so much to offer the Lord! In fact, I (Chris) still cringe when I hear a person say, "Wouldn't it be great if so-in-so got saved. They would really be an asset to the Lord." No matter how prominent we are or what we may have become, we must all "deny ourselves, pick up our cross and follow Jesus," if we are to be absolutely surrendered to Him. We must let Jesus lead, so we can follow. We can't be so hard on Peter. He was just thinking in his flesh, for that was all he knew at that time. And, that is all many Christians still know! Let's look upon each other with the eyes of love and pray for each other. Let's pray we can all get to the end of ourselves. Although this is often not an easy or comfortable place to be brought to, it is also a glorious place of new beginnings with Jesus.

# CHAPTER 5

## *Impossible with Man, Possible with God*

> But He said, "The things which are impossible with men
> are possible with God." Luke 18:27

IN LUKE 18:18-27, JESUS HAD SAID TO THE RICH YOUNG RULER, "SELL ALL THAT you have...and come, follow Me." The young man went away sorrowful. Jesus then turned to his disciples and said, "How hard it is for those who have riches to enter the kingdom of God." The disciples, we read, were greatly astonished, and answered, "Who, then, can be saved?" Jesus gave this blessed answer, "The things which are impossible with men are possible with God."

This passage of scripture contains two great lessons every person needs to learn in the Christian life. It often takes a long time to learn the first lesson: that in salvation and following Jesus by living a holy life, it is impossible for man to do it. Often a man learns this and yet he does not learn the second lesson - what is impossible with man is possible with God. Blessed is the man who learns both lessons! The learning of them can mark stages in the Christian life.

## Man Cannot

One stage is when a person is trying to do his utmost and fails. Then, he tries to do better and fails again. Still, he tries much more and he always fails. And yet, very often he does not even then learn the lesson: with man it is impossible to serve God and Jesus. People may spend years serving the Lord and have never learned that it is impossible until they reach a point of utter despair and exhaustion. And then they learn it. Peter spent three years in Christ's school, and he never learned it is impossible until he denied his Lord, went out, and wept bitterly. Then he learned it.

Just look for a moment at a person who is learning this lesson. At first, he fights against it. Then, he submits to it, but reluctantly and in despair. At last, he accepts it willingly and rejoices in it. At the beginning of the Christian life, the young convert has no conception of this truth. He has been converted and has the joy of the Lord in his heart, so he begins to run the race and fight the battle. He is sure he can conquer for he is zealous and honest, and God will help him. Yet, somehow, very soon there is failure where he did not expect it, and sin gets the better of him. Disappointed, he may think, "I was not watchful enough and I did not make my resolutions strong enough." He may make another vow, pray again, and yet fail again. He may even get to the point where he asks himself, "Am I really saved? Do I really have the life of God within me?" Eventually, he thinks, "Yes. I know I am saved. I have Jesus Christ to help me. I can live the holy life."

At a later period, he comes to another state of mind. He begins to see such a life is impossible, but he does not accept it. He may even think to himself, "Since I cannot, God doesn't really expect me to do what I cannot do." When he realizes that God does expect it, it is a mystery to him. This is the time he is tempted to quit trying. This is where many Christians are living a low life -a life of failure and sin - instead of a life of rest and victory because they say, "I cannot. It is impossible." And yet they do not understand it fully. So, under the impression I cannot, they give way to despair. They will do their best, but they never expect to get very far.

But God leads His children on to a third stage in which we realize, "I must do it, and I will do it. It is impossible for man, and yet I must do it." The renewed will begins to exercise its whole power, and in intense longing and prayer begins to cry to God, "Lord, what is the meaning of this? How am I to be freed from the power of sin?"

It is the state of the regenerate man in Romans Chapter 7. There we find the Christian man trying his very best to live a holy life. God's law has been revealed to him as reaching down into the very depth of the desires

40

of the heart. The man can dare to say, "I delight in the law of God after the inward man. To will what is good is present within me. My heart loves the law of God, and my will has chosen that law."

Can a man like that fail, with his heart full of delight in God's law and with his will determined to do what is right? The answer is yes. This is what Romans Chapter 7 teaches us. There is something more needed. Not only must I delight in the law of God after the inward man and will what God wills, but I need divine omnipotence to work it in me. That is what the apostle Paul teaches in Philippians 2:13: "For it is God who works in you both to will and to do for His good pleasure."

Note the contrast. In Romans Chapter 7, the saved man says, "To will is present with me, but to do that which is good, I cannot" (Romans 7:18). But in Philippians Chapter 2, you have a man who has been led on farther. He is a man who understands that when God has worked the renewed will, God will give the power to accomplish what that will desires. Let us receive this as one of the first great lessons in our spiritual life: "It is impossible for me, my God. Let there be an end of the flesh and all its powers, an end of self-will, and let it be my glory to be helpless." Praise God for His divine teaching that makes us helpless!

When you thought of absolute surrender to God, were you not brought to an end of yourself? May you learn the lesson now. If you felt you could not do it, you are on the right road, if you let yourself be led. Accept this position, and maintain it before God: "My heart's desire and delight, Oh God, is absolute surrender, but I cannot perform it. It is impossible for me to live that life. It is beyond me." Kneel before God and learn that when you are utterly helpless, God will come to work in you not only to will, but also to do.

## God Can

Now comes the second lesson. "The things which are impossible with men are possible with God." Beware of the temptation of giving up before the Lord works this in you. Unfortunately, there are many Christians who have learned the lesson, "it is impossible with men," and then give up in helpless despair. They live a frustrated Christian life without joy, strength, or victory. Why? It is because they do not humble themselves to learn the other lesson: with God all things are possible.

Your Christian life is to be a continuous proof that God works impossibilities! Your Christian life is to be a series of impossibilities made possible and actual by God's almighty power. That is what every Christian needs. Unfortunately, many Christians believe they only need a little of God's power, but in actuality, it's the whole of God's omnipotent power needed to keep us right and to live the Christian life.

The whole of Christianity is based on God's ability to make the impossible become possible. It is a work of God's omnipotence. For example, the birth of Jesus was a miracle of divine power. Remember the angel said to Mary, "For with God nothing will be impossible" (Luke 1:37). Also, Christ's resurrection could never have happened without God's omnipotence. We are taught that it was according to the exceeding greatness of His mighty power that God raised Christ from the dead.

Every tree must grow on the root from which it springs. An oak tree 300 years old grows all the time on the one root from which it had its beginning. Remember that in the beginning God created something out of nothing, proving that Christianity had its beginning in the omnipotence of God. In every soul, Christianity must have its continuance in that omnipotence. All the possibilities of a higher Christian life have their origin in a new understanding of Christ's power to work all God's will in us.

May we all come and worship our almighty God! Have you learned to do it? Have you learned to deal so closely with your almighty God that you know omnipotence is working in you? In outward appearance there is often little sign of it. The apostle Paul said, "I was with you in weakness and in fear and in much trembling, and …my preaching was… in demonstration of the Spirit and of power" (1 Corinthians 2:3-4). From the human side there was feebleness. From the divine side there was divine omnipotence. And that is true of every godly life. If we would only learn that lesson better, and give a wholehearted, undivided surrender to it, we would learn what blessedness there is in dwelling every hour and every moment with an almighty God. Have you ever studied in the Bible the attribute of God's omnipotence? You know that it was God's omnipotence that created the world, created light out of darkness, and created man. But have you studied God's omnipotence in the works of redemption?

Look at Abraham. When God called him to be the father of that people from which Christ was to be born, God said to him, "I am God Almighty, walk before me and be thou perfect" (Genesis 17:1, KJV). And God trained Abraham to trust Him as the omnipotent One. Abraham trusted God when he was going out to a new land he did not know, and he had faith to say, "This is my land," when he was a pilgrim amidst thousands of Canaanites. Whether he was waiting 25 years for a son in his old age against all hope, or obediently offering up Isaac on Mt. Moriah, Abraham believed God. He was strong in faith, giving glory to God, because he accounted Him who had promised able to perform. "He did not waver at the promise of God through unbelief, but was strengthened in faith, giving glory to God, and being fully convinced that what He had promised He was also able to perform" (Romans 4:20-21).

The cause of the weakness of your Christian life is that you want to work it out partly, and to let God help you. And that cannot be. You must come to be utterly helpless, to let God work. And God will work gloriously. It is this that we need if we indeed are to be used mightily of God. Scripture proves how Moses, when he led Israel out of Egypt; how Joshua, when he brought them into the land of Canaan; and how all God's servants in the Old Testament counted on the omnipotence of God doing impossibilities.

And this God lives today, and this God is the God of every child of His. And yet some of us want God to give us a little help while we do our best, instead of coming to understand what God wants, and to say, "I can do nothing. God must and will do all." In work, in sanctification, in obedience to God, in all I do, I can do nothing of myself. Therefore, my place is to worship our omnipotent God and believe He will work in me every moment. Oh, may God teach us this! Oh, that God would by His grace show you what a God you have, and to what an omnipotent God you have entrusted yourself. He is willing, with His whole omnipotence, to place Himself at the disposal of every child of His! Will we not take the lesson of the Lord Jesus, and say, "Amen! The things which are impossible with men are possible with God?"

Remember Peter's self-confidence, self-power, self-will, and how he came to deny his Lord. You may feel, "Ah! There is the self-life; there is the flesh-life that rules in me!" And now, have you believed that there is deliverance from that? Have you believed that Almighty God is able to reveal Jesus Christ in your heart, to let the Holy Spirit rule in you so that the self-life shall not have power or dominion over you? Have you coupled the two together, and with deep humiliation cried out, "Oh, Lord God, it is impossible to me; man cannot do it, but glory to Your name, it is possible with You?" Have you claimed deliverance? Do it now. Put yourself afresh in absolute surrender into the hands of God who infinitely loves you. It will be one of the most freeing things you will ever do. As His love is infinite, so is His power to do it.

## Sanctification: God Works in Man

Once again, we come to the question of absolute surrender, as it appears to be lacking in the body of Christ. This is why the Holy Spirit cannot fill us, and why we cannot live as people entirely separated unto the Holy Spirit. This is why the flesh and self-life cannot be conquered. We have not yet understood what it is to be absolutely surrendered to God as Jesus was. Many Christians honestly and whole-heartedly say, "Amen. I accept the message of absolute surrender to God." Yet they question, "Will that ever be mine? Can I count upon God to make me a Christian of whom it is said, 'He lives in absolute surrender to God?'" Brother, sister, "The things which are impossible with men are possible with God." Do believe that, when Jesus Christ takes charge of you, He can make you a person of absolute surrender. And God is able to maintain that. He is able to let you rise every morning of the week with the blessed thought either directly or indirectly, "I am in God's charge. My God is working out my life for me."

Many may be weary thinking about sanctification. Some have prayed, cried, and longed to be sanctified, and yet, it appears so far off! They are so conscious of how distant the holiness and humility of Jesus is. Beloved friend, the one doctrine of sanctification that is scriptural, real, and effective is: "The things which are impossible with men are possible with God." God can sanctify men. By His almighty and sanctifying power, every moment God can keep us. Oh, that we might get a step nearer to our God now! Oh, that the light of God might shine, and that we might know our God better!

Think about the life of Christ in us – living like Jesus, receiving Jesus Christ as our Savior from sin, and as our life and strength. It is God in heaven who can reveal that in you. The apostle Paul prayed, "That He would grant you according to His riches in glory to be strengthened with might by His Spirit in the inner man" (Ephesians 3:16). Do you see that we have an omnipotent God working by His omnipotence in the heart of His believing children, so that Jesus can become an indwelling Savior? You may have tried to grasp it, understand it, and to believe it, yet it would not come. It is because you still do not grasp that "the things which are impossible with men, are possible with God."

Also, the word previously mentioned about love may have brought many to see that we must have an inflow of love in quite a new way. Our heart must be filled with life from above, from the Fountain of everlasting love, if it is going to overflow all day. Then, it will be just as natural for us to love our fellowmen as it is natural for the lamb to be gentle. If these words bring us to say, "This is a love utterly beyond my power," then we understand "it is absolutely impossible" for me. Then, we can come to God and say, "It is possible with You." Just as we recognize we cannot save ourselves, but need the saving power of Christ, also we must realize that we need the loving power of Jesus in order to genuinely love the unlovable. **Note: This is not in any way condoning abusive behavior of any sort or staying in any sort of abuse. If you are in any abuse, please be safe and prayerfully seek help and guidance!**

Many of us are crying to God for a great revival. This is the unceasing prayer of our hearts, as well. Oh, if God would only revive His believing people first. Thousands of Christians yearn for holiness and consecration. It is a forerunner of God's power. God works to will, and then He works to do. These yearnings are a proof that God has worked to will in us. Let us have faith to believe that God will work to do among His people more than we can ask. Paul said, "Now to Him who is able to do exceedingly abundantly above all that we ask or think, according to the power that works in us, to Him be glory" (Ephesians 3:20-21a). Let our hearts say that. Glory to God, the omnipotent One, who can do above what we dare to ask or think!

"The things which are impossible with men are possible with God." All around us there is a world of sin and sorrow, and the Devil is there. But remember, Christ is on the throne, Christ is stronger, Christ has conquered, and Christ will conquer! So, wait on God. "Things are impossible with men" may cast us down, but ultimately we are lifted up with "are possible with God." Get linked to God. Adore and trust Him as the omnipotent One, not only for your own life, but for all the people who are entrusted to you. Always pray adoring His omnipotence by saying, "Almighty God, I claim Your Almightiness." You will find that the answer to your prayer will come. Like Abraham you will become strong in faith, giving glory to God, because you account Him who has promised able to perform.

**Points to Ponder:**

If God has used His unlimited power to do everything He has done since the beginning of the universe, why would we think He would expect us to do HIS work in any other way? In other words, why would our Heavenly Father expect us to do His will in our power? He wouldn't and He doesn't. He is not a heavy taskmaster. If what is before you is too hard for you, it is not too hard for Jesus. Spend some time with Him and rest for a while in His precious, loving presence, praising Him that, "What is impossible with man is possible with God." He is a completely loving God graciously offering us a completely loving relationship with Him. "Come to Me, all you who labor and are heavy laden, and I will give you rest. Take My yoke upon you and learn from Me, for I am gentle and lowly in heart, and you will find rest for your souls. For My yoke is easy and My burden is light." (Matthew 11:28-30).

# CHAPTER 6

## Who Will Deliver Me?

"O wretched man that I am! Who will deliver me from this body of death? I thank God—through Jesus Christ our Lord!" Romans 7:24-25a

YOU KNOW THE WONDERFUL LOCATION THAT THIS TEXT HAS IN THE EPISTLE TO the Romans. It stands at the end of Romans Chapter 7, and is the gateway to Chapter 8. Notice that the Holy Spirit is mentioned 16 times in the first 16 verses of Chapter 8. There you have the description and promise of the life that a child of God can live in the power of the Holy Spirit. This begins in the second verse: "The law of the Spirit of life in Christ Jesus has made me free from the law of sin and death" (Romans 8:2). From that, Paul goes on to speak of the great privileges of the child of God who is to be led by the Spirit of God. The gateway into all this is found at the end of Chapter 7: "O wretched man that I am!" Here are the words of a man who has come to the end of himself. He has in the previous verses described how he had struggled and wrestled in his own power to obey the holy law of God, and had failed. But in answer to his own questions, he now finds the true answer and cries out, "I thank God through Jesus Christ our Lord!" From that, he goes on to speak of what that deliverance is that he has found.

Romans 8:15 reads, "For you did not receive the spirit of bondage again to fear." We are continually warned that this is a great danger of the Christian life: to again go into bondage. In order to understand the path unto which a man may be led out of the spirit of bondage into the glorious liberty of the children of God, let's look at the four stages this man travels, found in the book of Romans. First, the words are the language of a regenerate man; second, of a weak man; third, of a wretched man; and fourth, of a man on the border of complete liberty.

## The Regenerate Man

In Romans 7:17, he declares, "It is no more I that do it, but sin that dwells in me." That is the language of a regenerate man - a man who knows that his heart and nature have been renewed, and that sin is now a power in him that is not himself. "I delight in the law of the Lord after the inward man" (Romans 7:22). That again is the language of a regenerate man. He dares to say when he does evil, "It is no more I that do it, but sin that dwells in me" (Romans 7:17). It is of great importance to understand this.

In the first five chapters of Romans, Paul deals with justification and sanctification. In dealing with justification, he lays the foundation of the doctrine in the teaching about sin - the actual transgressions, or otherwise, actions. In the second part of the fifth chapter, he begins to deal with sin, not as actual transgression, but as a power. Thank the Lord that Paul did not omit the vital teaching of the sinfulness of the believer. We would have missed the answer to the question we all have about sinfulness in the believer. So, what is the answer? The regenerate man is one in whom the will has been renewed, and who can say, "I delight in the law of God after the inward man."

## The Weak Man

Here is a great mistake made by many Christian people: they think that since they have a renewed will, it is enough. But this is not the case. This regenerate man tells us, "I will to do what is good, but the power to perform I find not" (Romans 7:18b). Even the determined man fails. Often people tell us, "If you just set your mind to it, you can perform it." But this man was as determined as any man can be, and yet he made the confession,

"To will is present with me; but how to perform that which is good, I find not" (Romans 7:18b). But you ask, "How is it God makes a regenerate man utter such a confession?" After all, he possesses a right will, with a heart that longs to do good, and hungers to do his very best to love God.

Let's look at this question: What has God given us our will for? Even the angels who fell could not stand in their own strength and will. The will of man is nothing but an empty vessel in which the power of God is to be made manifest. Man must seek in God all that is to be. You have it in Philippians 2:13, and you have it here also, that God's work is to work in us both to will and to do of His good pleasure. Here is a man who appears to have the will, but is saying, "God has not worked the 'to do' in me." But we are taught that God works both to will and to do. How is the apparent contradiction to be reconciled? How do we get to the point that we not only will it, but are also able to do it, since God works both to will and to do?

In Romans 7:6-25, notice the name of the Holy Spirit does not occur once, nor does the name of Jesus occur. The man is wrestling and struggling to fulfill God's law. Instead of the Holy Spirit and Jesus, the law is mentioned nearly 20 times. In this chapter, it shows a believer doing his very best to obey the law of God with his regenerate will. Not only this, but you will find the three little words "I", "me", and "my" occur more than 40 times. It is the regenerate "I" in its weakness seeking to obey the law without being filled with the Holy Spirit. This is the experience of almost every Christian. After conversion, a man begins to do his best, and fails. But there is no need at all to fail if we are yielded to the Holy Spirit.

God allows this failure so that the regenerate man may be taught his own utter inability. It is in the course of this struggle that the sense of our utter sinfulness comes to us. God allows man to strive to fulfill the law so that, as he strives and wrestles, he may be brought to this, "I am a regenerate child of God, but I am completely helpless to obey His law in my flesh." Look at the strong words Paul uses in this chapter to describe this condition: "I am carnal, sold under sin" (Romans 7:14). He goes on to say, "I see another law in my members bringing me into captivity" (Romans 7:23). Last of all, Paul writes, "O wretched man that I am! Who will deliver me from this body of death" (Romans 7:24)? This believer who bows here in deep contrition is utterly unable to obey the law of God in and of himself alone.

## The Wretched Man

Not only is the man who makes this confession a regenerate and a weak man, but he is also a wretched man. He is utterly unhappy and miserable. What is it that makes him so thoroughly miserable? It is because God has given him a nature that loves God. He is deeply wretched because he knows he is not obeying his God whom he loves. He says, with brokenness of heart, "It is not I that does it, but I am under the awful power of sin which is holding me down. It is I, and yet not I - it is myself so closely bound up with my sinful nature." Blessed be God when a man learns to say, "O wretched man that I am!" in sincerity from the depth of his heart. Hallelujah! He is on the way to Chapter 8 of Romans.

There are many who make this confession a pillow for sin. They say that if Paul had to confess his weakness and helplessness in this way, how can they do any better? So, the call to holiness may be quietly set aside. May it not be so with us! Pray that every one of us would learn to say these words in the very spirit in which they are written here! May God help us when we sin to take this verse to heart! If ever we utter a sharp word, may we say, "O wretched man that I am!" Furthermore, every time we lose our temper, may we kneel down and understand that God never meant His child to remain in this state. If only we would take this word into our daily life, and say it every time we are disturbed about our own honor! If only we would take it into our hearts every time we sin against our Lord! God, help us to forget everything else and cry out, "O wretched man that I am! Who will deliver me from this body of death? I thank God through Jesus Christ our Lord!"

Why should you say this whenever you commit sin? You should say it because it is when a man is brought to this confession that deliverance is at hand. Also remember, it was not only the sense of being weak and taken captive that made him wretched. Above all, it was the sense of sinning against his God! The law was doing its work, making sin exceedingly sinful in his sight. The thought of continually grieving God became utterly unbearable. It was this that brought forth the piercing cry: "O wretched man!" As long as we talk and reason about our inability and our failure, and only try to find out what Romans Chapter 7 means, it will profit us little. But once every sin gives new intensity to our sense of wretchedness, and we feel our whole state as one of not only helplessness, but actual exceeding sinfulness, we will be pressed not only to ask: "Who shall deliver us," but to cry: "I thank God through Jesus Christ my Lord."

## The Almost Delivered Man

The man in our passage has tried repeatedly to obey God's law. He has loved it. He has wept over his sin and he has tried to conquer. He has tried to overcome fault after fault, yet every time he has ended in failure. We have to ask ourselves, what did Paul mean when he said, "This body of death?" He didn't mean our bodies when we die. He gives the answer to what he means in Romans 8:13b (KJV): "If ye through the Spirit do mortify the deeds of the body, ye shall live." The deeds (our sinful natures) are the body of death from which he is seeking deliverance. Our sinful deeds need to go - by first, recognizing our captivity. Now he is on the brink of deliverance.

In Romans 7:23, we have these words: "I see another law in my members, warring against the law of my mind, and bringing me into captivity to the law of sin which is in my members." It is a captive that cries, "O wretched man that I am! Who will deliver me from this body of death?" He is a man who knows in his heart that he is bound, helpless, and in need of deliverance. But, in Romans 8:2, there is a complete contrast to his hopelessness. Here is where Paul speaks of redemption from self: "The law of the Spirit of life in Christ Jesus has made me FREE from the law of sin and death" (Romans 8:2, Emphasis ours). That is the deliverance through Jesus Christ our Lord - the liberty to the captive which the Spirit brings. You cannot keep captive any longer a man who has been made free by the "law of the Spirit of life in Christ Jesus!" Even though the regenerate man in chapter six of Romans had the Spirit of Jesus, he had not yet come to understand what the Holy Spirit could do for him. He always had God's Spirit, but he did not realize or know the Spirit's power! The darkness of ignorance cannot put out the truth or light, but it can cover it.

When God works in His people, He leads His people on as reasonable, intelligent beings. Therefore, when He wants to fill us with the Holy Spirit, he first brings us to the end of ourselves. He brings us to the conviction that though we have been striving to obey the law, we have failed. When we get to that point, He shows us that in the Holy Spirit we have the power of obedience, the power of victory, and the power of real holiness. God works to will, and He is ready to work to do, but many Christians misunderstand this. They think because they have the will, it is enough, and that now they are able to do. This is not so. The new will is a permanent gift, an attribute of the new nature. The power to do is not a permanent gift. This is a choice that must be made moment by moment and it must be received from the Holy Spirit. It is the man who is conscious of his own weakness as a believer who will learn that only by the Holy Spirit can he live a holy life. This man is on the brink of that great deliverance! The way has been prepared for the man to enter into the glorious Chapter 8 of Romans.

Beloved, where are you living? Is it, "O wretched man that I am! Who shall deliver me?" with now and then a little experience of the power of the Holy Spirit? Or is it, "I thank God through Jesus Christ! The law of the Spirit has set me free from the law of sin and death?" It is the Holy Spirit who gives the victory. It is He who, when the heart is open wide to receive Him, comes in and reigns there and mortifies the deeds of the body day by day, hour by hour, and moment by moment.

Let's bring this to a point. Remember, dear friend, what we need is to come to a decision and an action. There are in Scripture two very different types of Christians: those who yield to the flesh and those who yield to the Holy Spirit. The Bible speaks in Romans, Corinthians, and Galatians about yielding to the flesh, and that is the life of many believers. These Christians live in lack of joy and liberty because they are living in the flesh. The Spirit is within them, but the flesh rules their lives. To be led by the Spirit of God is what they need. Heavenly Father, help us realize what it means that You, the everlasting God, have given Your dear Son, Jesus Christ, to watch over us every day, and that what we have to do is to trust. Help us realize that the work of the Holy Spirit is to enable us every moment to remember Jesus, and to trust Him! The Spirit has come to keep the link with Him unbroken every moment. Praise God for the Holy Spirit! We are so accustomed to thinking of the Holy Spirit as a luxury, for special times, or for special pastors or missionaries. But the Holy Spirit is necessary for every believer, every moment of the day. Praise God you have Him, and that He gives you the full experience of the deliverance in Christ as He makes you free from the power of sin.

Who longs to have the power and the freedom of the Holy Spirit? May we bow before God in a cry of despair, "Oh God, must I go on sinning this way forever? Who shall deliver me?" Thank God through Jesus Christ for He shall deliver me. This deliverance happens when we are ready to sink before God, yield, and seek the power of Jesus to dwell and work in us. Are you ready to say, "I thank God through Jesus Christ?

What good does it do that we go to church or attend conventions, that we study our Bibles and pray, unless our lives are filled with the Holy Spirit? That is what God wants. Nothing else will enable us to live a life of power and peace. If you want the path to full deliverance of Jesus, and the liberty of the Spirit, take it through the seventh chapter of Romans. Then say, "I thank God through Jesus Christ our Lord. Even though I do not see it all or understand it all, I am going to praise God." There is deliverance. There is the freedom of the Holy Spirit. "For the kingdom of God is… righteousness and peace and joy in the Holy Spirit" (Romans 14:17).

**Points to Ponder:**

The beautiful way the Lord works is through the change the Holy Spirit does within us. Many times the work is already accomplished and we don't even know it. This changing from within is exactly the opposite of the method we try to do. We usually try to force the changes from the outside in. Remember, it's not possible for us to accomplish His work in us. We can, however, sometimes be successful in changing the outside, but if the inside isn't changed, what is inside will eventually come out! Paul asks, "Where is the boasting in that?" Boasting is excluded because what I was, a fallen sinner, I still am. It is only when we yield to the Holy Spirit within us that we are conformed into the image of Jesus Christ. Our old nature has less power and His new nature is formed in us. Will we sin again? Yes, but in that failure there is hope, for the Lord is able to work in us with His power and His will. In one area after another in our life, yielding to the power of Christ, we will begin to experience real changes; thus, the conformity to the image of our Lord Jesus Christ. Spend some time in prayer with your loving Savior confessing your sins and let Him cleanse you. "If we confess our sins, He is faithful and just to forgive us our sins and to cleanse us from all unrighteousness" (1 John 1:9). He truly desires to change us into His beautiful image. Are you willing to allow Him to do this?

# CHAPTER 7

## *Having Begun in the Spirit*

"This only I want to learn from you: Did you receive the Spirit by the works of the law, or by the hearing of faith? Are you so foolish? Having begun in the Spirit, are you now being made perfect by the flesh?" Galatians 3:2-3

WHEN SPEAKING OF THE QUICKENING, DEEPENING, OR STRENGTHENING OF THE spiritual life, people are thinking of something that is powerless, wrong, and sinful. It is a great thing to take our place before God with the confession: "Oh God, our spiritual life is not what it should be!" May God work that in our hearts!

Unfortunately, there are many indications of powerlessness, failure, sin, and shortcomings in many Christian's lives. This compels us to ask: Why is it? Is there any necessity for Christians to be living in such a low state? Or is it actually possible that God's people could be living in the joy and strength of their God? Surely, every believing heart must answer: It is possible! Why, then, are many Christians living in this powerless state? There must be a reason for this. Has God not given Jesus Christ, His Almighty Son, to be the Keeper of every believer, to make Him an ever-present reality in our lives daily, and to impart and communicate to us all that we have in Jesus? God has given us His Son, and God has given us His Spirit. How is it that we, as believers, do not live up to our privileges and in our freedoms that Jesus gave us with His death and resurrection?

In more than one of the epistles, we find a very solemn answer to that question. There are epistles such as the first to the Thessalonians, where Paul writes to the Christians, in effect, "I want you to grow, to abound, to increase more and more." They were young, and there were things lacking in their faith. But Paul had such great joy in that their state was so notably satisfactory. Yet, there are other epistles where he takes a very different tone. In his epistles to the Corinthians and Galatians, Paul tells them in many different ways the one reason they were not living as Christians ought to live. Many of them were living under the power of the flesh. Paul reminds them that by the preaching of faith they had received the Holy Spirit. He had preached Jesus Christ to them; they had accepted Jesus and had received the Holy Spirit in power. But what happened? Having begun in the Spirit, they tried to perfect the work that the Spirit had begun in the flesh by their own effort.

Now, we have here a solemn discovery of what the great need is in believers. God has called us to live in the power of the Holy Spirit. But many Christians live, for the most part, in the power of human flesh, and of will, energy, and effort apart from the Spirit of God. Oh Beloved, here is the main message of these writings: If we will return to acknowledge that the Holy Spirit is our strength and our help; if we will surrender everything into Jesus' hands and wait to be led by the Holy Spirit, our days of beauty and gladness will return. Then, we will see the glory of God revealed among us. Nothing will help us unless we come to understand that we must live every day under the power of the Holy Spirit. God wants us to be living vessels in whom the power of the Spirit is to be manifested every hour and every moment of our lives. God will enable us to be that.

Let us take hold of this great truth from Paul's word to the Galatians, which is actually quite simple. First, it shows us the beginning of the Christian life is in receiving the Holy Spirit as we accept Jesus into our hearts as Lord and Savior. Secondly, there is great danger in forgetting that we are to live, from that point on, in the guidance and power of the Holy Spirit, rather than living in our flesh. Thirdly, it shows us the fruits and the proofs of our seeking perfection in the flesh. Lastly, it suggests to us the way of deliverance from this fleshly state.

## Receiving the Holy Spirit

First, let us take hold of this great truth: The beginning of the true Christian life is to receive the Holy Spirit. And the work of every Christian minister is the same as was the work of Paul: to remind his people that they received the Holy Spirit, and must live according to His guidance and in His power.

If those Galatians who received the Holy Spirit in power were tempted to go astray by that terrible danger of perfecting in the flesh what had begun in the Spirit, how much more danger do those Christians run who hardly recognize they have received the Holy Spirit! How much more danger is there for those who hardly ever think of the gift of the Holy Spirit, and hardly ever praise God for it!

## Neglecting the Holy Spirit

Let's look at this great danger using the example of a train. A train may be traveling in a certain direction, and the points at some place along the tracks may not be properly opened or closed, so that unobservantly the train is switched off to the right or to the left. If this takes place, for instance, on a dark night, the train goes in the wrong direction, and the people might not know it until they have gone quite a distance.

Just so, God gives Christians the Holy Spirit with the intention that every day is to be lived in the power of the Holy Spirit. A man cannot live one hour of a godly life unless by the power of the Holy Spirit. He may live a proper, consistent, irreproachable life, and a life of virtue and diligent service. But, to live a life acceptable to God, in the enjoyment of God's salvation and His love, and to live and walk in the power of the new life, he cannot do it unless he lives in the power and guidance of the Holy Spirit every day and every hour.

Here is the danger. We saw it in the Galatians walk and we see it in our own walk. What was begun by the Spirit we try to perfect in the flesh. How did it happen to the Galatians? They began listening to the Judiazing teachers, who told them they must be circumcised. These practices made their relationship with God about external observances. Therefore, Paul uses this expression about those teachers who had them circumcised "so that they may boast in your flesh" (Galatians 6:13).

Our human nature, human will, and self-efforts can be very active in our Christian walk. Although we may be converted and have received the Holy Spirit, still we may begin in our own strength to try to serve God. I may be very diligent and doing a great deal, and yet all the time it is more the work of the human flesh than of God's Spirit. What a solemn thought that man can, without noticing, be switched off from the line of the Holy Spirit onto the line of the flesh.

How solemn it is that man can be most diligent and make great sacrifices, and yet it is all in the power of the human will. Ah, the great question for us to ask of God in self-examination is that we may be shown whether our Christian life is lived more in the power of the flesh than in the power of the Holy Spirit. A man may be a pastor or missionary who works most diligently in his ministry or a man may be a Christian worker of whom others say of him that he makes great sacrifices, and yet you can feel there is something lacking. You feel that he is not living in the power and under the guidance of the Holy Spirit. How many Christians there are about whom the same can be said. Ah! There is the weakness of the believer. It is all in that one word – flesh.

The flesh may manifest itself in many ways. It may be manifested in fleshly wisdom. My mind may be most active about Christianity. I may preach, teach, write, think, or meditate, and even delight in being occupied with things in God's Word or in Christian work. Yet, the power of the Holy Spirit may be markedly absent. Why is there sometimes little converting power in the preaching of the Word? Why is there so much work and often so little result for eternity? Why, at times, does the Word have so little power to build up believers in holiness and consecration? It is the absence of the power of the Holy Spirit. And why is this? There can be no other reason except that the flesh and human energy have taken the place that the Holy Spirit ought to have. It was true of the Galatians and the Corinthians. You know Paul said to them, "I could not speak to you as to spiritual people, but as to carnal" (1 Corinthians 3:1). Also, you know how often in the course of his epistle he had to reprove and condemn them for strife and divisions.

## Lacking the Fruit of the Holy Spirit

A third thought is, "What are the proofs or indications that a Christian is serving God in the power of the flesh – is perfecting in the flesh what was begun in the Spirit?" The answer is very easy. Religious self-effort always ends in sinful flesh. What was the state of those Galatians? They were striving to be justified by the works of the law. And yet they were quarreling and in danger of devouring one another. Count the number of expressions the apostle uses to indicate their lack of love. There are more than twelve, including envy, jealousy, bitterness, strife, and others. In the fourth and fifth chapters, we see how they tried to serve God in their own strength and utterly failed. All this religious effort resulted in failure. The power of sin and the sinful flesh got the better of them. Even though we don't see it at the time, learning to walk in the Spirit sometimes comes from failing in the flesh.

There are often complaints of the lack of a high standard of integrity and godliness, even among professing believers. Think of the life to which God has called His children, and which He enables them to live by the Holy Spirit. In the homes of Christians, is there often unlovingness, temper, sharpness, and bitterness? Think how often there is envy, jealousy, sensitiveness, or pride among the members of churches. Then, we are compelled to ask, "Where are marks of the presence of the Spirit of the Lamb of God?"

Many people speak of these things as though they were the natural result of our weakness and cannot be helped. Many people speak of these things as sins, yet have given up the hope of conquering them. They do not see the least prospect of ever having the things changed. There is no prospect until the Christian begins to see that every sin in him comes from the flesh – from a fleshly life in the midst of our Christian activities, from a striving in self-effort to serve God. We will fail until we learn to make confession, and until we begin to see that we must continually yield to the Holy Spirit. If we are yielded to the Holy Spirit, we will not serve God with self-effort. May we study God's Word to discover the truth about the Holy Spirit and how to walk in His power! May we confess that we have grieved the Holy Spirit by trying to live a godly life with as little as possible of God's Spirit! May we seek after Him with our whole heart!

All the weakness in believers is because of our refusal to obey God. And why is that so? Many will answer, "We are too weak and too helpless. We vow to obey, but somehow we fail." Ah, yes, we fail because we do not accept the strength of God. God alone can work out His will in us. We cannot work out God's will, but His Holy Spirit can. Until believers grasp this, and stop trying by human effort to do God's will, and wait upon the Holy Spirit and His omnipotent, enabling power to come, we will never be what God wants us to be and what God is willing to make of us.

## Yielding to the Holy Spirit

Lastly, what is the way to restoration? Beloved friend, the answer is simple. If that train has been switched off, there is nothing for it to do but to go back to the point at which it was led away. The Galatians had no other way in returning but to come back to where they had gone wrong. They had to come back from all religious effort in their own strength, from seeking anything by their own work, and to yield themselves humbly to the Holy Spirit. There is no other way for us as individuals.

Are you a brother or sister whose heart is conscious of this thought, "My life knows little of the power of the Holy Spirit?" God's message is that you can have no conception of what your life would be in the power of the Holy Spirit except through the experience of it. It is too high, too blessed, and too wonderful to describe in human words. But just as truly as the everlasting Jesus came to this world, did His wonderful works, died and rose again to bring about our redemption by His precious blood, so can the Holy Spirit come into your heart. With His divine power, He can sanctify you and enable you to do God's blessed will, as well as fill your heart with joy and strength. But, we have forgotten, we have grieved, and we have dishonored the Holy Spirit; and He has not been able to do His work. The Father in heaven loves to give His children His Holy Spirit. God longs to give each person individually, separately, the power of the Holy Spirit for daily life. God wants us, as His children, to arise and place our sins before Him. He wants us to call on Him for mercy. Forgive us, Lord, for forgetting, grieving, and dishonoring the Holy Spirit. Forgive us for trying to perfect in the flesh what was begun in the Spirit. We bow and confess before You, Lord how our fleshly religion, our self-effort, and self-confidence have been the cause of every failure. Help us live under the power of the Holy Spirit day by day, moment by moment. By Your power, may we show people what a life lived under the power of the Holy Spirit looks like, not only in our words and teaching, but in the lives we live every day. Heavenly Father, help us to do it!

Many times people ask, "Why is it that I am failing? I have tried with my whole heart and I desire to serve God." The answer is, "My dear friends, you are trying to do in your own strength what Jesus Christ alone can do in you." They may argue, "I'm sure I knew Christ alone could do it. I was not trusting in myself." The answer is, "You were trusting in yourself or you could not have failed. If you had trusted Christ, He could not fail." Oh, this perfecting in the flesh what was begun in the Spirit runs deeper through us than we know! Let us ask God to show us that it is only when we are brought to utter repentance and emptiness that we are prepared to receive the blessing that comes from on high.

Now, a few questions: Are you living under the power of the Holy Spirit day by day and moment by moment? Or are you attempting to live without that? Remember, you cannot. Are you consecrated, given up to the Holy Spirit to work in you and to live in you? Oh, let's come and confess every failure of temper and every failure of tongue, however small. May we confess every failure due to the absence of the Holy Spirit and the presence of the power of self. Are you consecrated to God? Are you given up to the Holy Spirit? If your answer is no, Are you willing to be consecrated? Are you willing to give yourself up to the power of the Holy Spirit? You well know that the human side of consecration will not help you. I may dedicate myself a hundred times with all the intensity of my being, and that will not help me. What will help me is this: that God from heaven accepts and seals my consecration.

Are you now willing to give yourselves up to the Holy Spirit? You can do it now. A great deal of this may still be unclear, and beyond what we understand. You may feel nothing; but come. God alone can work the change. God alone, who gave us the Holy Spirit, can restore the Holy Spirit in power into our lives. God alone can "strengthen us with might by His Spirit in the inner man" (Ephesians 3:16). To every waiting heart that will make the sacrifice, give up everything, give time to cry and pray to God, the answer will come. The blessing is not far off. Our God delights in helping us. He will perfect, not in the flesh, but in the Spirit, what was begun in the Spirit. Hallelujah!

## Points to Ponder:

There are times when we start to panic because things aren't working out like we think they should. We're tempted to move ahead of the Lord and fix it ourselves! A good motto to remember is, "If there is frustration, there is flesh!" In these instances, we have left the foundation of belief in the Holy Spirit's ability to work in and through us, in order to complete the tasks He sets before us. The work the Lord has begun in us through the Holy Spirit cannot be perfected by the flesh. Spend some time with Jesus in worship and praise to Him. Delight yourself in Him. Spend time with Him in His Word and in prayer. You can trust Him to help you. May every one of us "live and move and have our being in Him" (Acts 17:28).

# CHAPTER 8

## *Kept By the Power of God Through Faith*

> "Blessed be the God and Father of our Lord Jesus Christ,
> who according to His abundant mercy has begotten us
> again to a living hope through the resurrection of Jesus
> Christ from the dead, to an inheritance incorruptible and
> undefiled and that does not fade away, reserved in heaven
> for you, who are kept by the power of God through faith
> for salvation ready to be revealed in the last time." 1 Peter
> 1:3-5

IN THIS SCRIPTURE WE HAVE TWO WONDERFUL, BLESSED TRUTHS ABOUT THE WAY a believer is kept unto salvation. One truth is, "Kept by the power of God"; and the other truth is, "Kept through faith." We have two sides: God's side and His almighty power, offered to us by our Keeper every moment of the day. On the human side, we have nothing to do but in faith to let God do His keeping work. We are begotten again to an inheritance kept in heaven for us. We are kept here on earth by the power of God.

We see there is double keeping: the inheritance kept for me in heaven and I on earth kept for the inheritance there. As for the first part of this keeping, there is no doubt and no question. God keeps the inheritance in heaven very wonderfully and perfectly, and it is waiting there safely. Also, the same God keeps me for the inheritance. This is what we want to understand. It is very foolish for a father to go to great trouble to have an inheritance for his children, and to keep it for them, if he does not keep them for it. Think of a man spending all of his time and making every sacrifice to amass a great amount of money. When you ask him why he sacrifices himself so, his answer is, "I want to leave my children a large inheritance, and I am keeping it for them." If you were then to hear that this man does not bother to educate his children, he allows them to run around in the street wild, and he does not intervene in their paths of sin, ignorance, and folly, what would you think of him? Would you not say, "Poor man! He is keeping an inheritance for his children, but he is not keeping or preparing his children for the inheritance!" There are so many Christians who think, "My God is keeping the inheritance for me." But, they cannot believe, "My God is keeping me for that inheritance." The same power, the same love, the same God is doing the double work. Here we have two truths: the divine side – we are kept by the power of God; the human side – we are kept through faith.

## Kept by the Power of God

Look at the divine side: Christians are kept by the power of God. God is keeping us for the inheritance. First, God's keeping includes all; it is all inclusive. What is kept? You are kept. How much of you? Your whole being is kept. Some people think of this as a sort of vague, general keeping; and that God will keep them in such a way that they will get to heaven. But they do not apply that word "kept" to everything in their being and nature. Yet, that is what God wants.

Many people have a watch. Suppose I borrow a watch from a friend and she says to me, "When you go to Europe, I will let you take it with you, but please keep it safe and bring it back to me." Suppose I damage the watch so that the face is cracked, the band is torn and dirty, and the internal mechanisms do not function properly. When I hand the watch to my friend in that condition, she would say, "Ah! But I gave you the watch on the condition that you would keep it." I could reply, "But I did keep it. Here is the watch." My friend would say, "But I did not want you to keep the watch in the general way, such that you would bring the watch back broken, dirty, and torn. I expected you to keep every part of it in good condition." Likewise, God does not want to keep us in this general way, so that at the last, somehow or other, we will be saved as by fire, and just get into heaven. Instead, the keeping power and the love of God apply to every part of our being.

There are some people who think God will keep them in spiritual things, but not in temporal things. The latter, they say, lies outside of His realm. Actually, God does send us to work in the world, but He did not say, "I must now leave you to go and earn your own money, and to get your livelihood for yourself." He knows you are not able to keep yourself. But God says, "My child, there is no work you are to do, no business in which you are engaged, and not a penny which you are to spend but I, your Father, will take that up into my keeping." God not only cares for the spiritual, but for the temporal, also. The greater part of many people's lives must be spent, sometime eight or ten hours a day, amid the temptations and distractions of their careers. But God will care for you there. The keeping of God includes all.

Some people say, "In a time of trial, God keeps me. But, when things are going well, I do not need His keeping. Then, I forget the Lord and let Him go." Conversely, there are people who say, "When things are smooth and going well, I am able to cling to God. But when heavy trials come, somehow or other my will rebels and I push the Lord away." In prosperity as in adversity, in the sunshine as in the dark, your God is ready to keep you all the time.

Also, people have a tendency to rate sins. They sometimes say, "The Lord may be concerned about bigger sins, but I cannot expect God to keep me from smaller sins. There is the sin of temper. I cannot expect God to conquer that! God is not so concerned about these little sins." Ah, but He is concerned about those. If God can keep you from falling into great sins, why do you not believe that He can keep you from outbreaks of temper? You thought that this was of less importance. You did not remember that the great commandment of the New Testament is: "Love one another as I have loved you" (John 13:34). When our temper, hasty judgements, or sharp words come out, we have sinned against Jesus' great commandment – the law of God's love. Yet, some may say, "God does not keep me from that." Others may say, "God can, but there is something in me that cannot attain to it, and which God does not take away."

Think about this: Can believers live a holier life than is generally lived? Can believers experience the keeping power of God in order to keep them from sin? Can believers be kept in fellowship with God? The answer comes in these words: "Kept by the power of God." The meaning is that if you will entrust yourself entirely and absolutely to the omnipotence of God, He will delight in keeping you. Let everyone who longs to live a holy life think about all their needs, their weaknesses, their shortcomings, and their sins, and say deliberately, "Is there any sin that my God cannot keep me from?" And the heart will have to answer, "No, God can keep me from any sin. But, I must remain yielded to the power of the Holy Spirit."

Secondly, God's keeping requires power. If you want to understand this keeping, remember that it is not only an all-inclusive keeping, but it is an almighty keeping. May I get that truth burned deep into my soul. May I worship God until my whole heart is filled with the thought of His omnipotence. God is almighty, and the Almighty God offers Himself to work in my heart to do the work of keeping me. I want to get linked to the omnipotent One, the Living God, and to have my place in the hollow of His hand. We read the Psalms, and we think of the wonderful thoughts in many of the expressions that David uses. For example, King David speaks about our God as our Fortress, our Refuge, our strong Tower, our Strength, and our Salvation. David had wonderful views of how the everlasting God is Himself the hiding place of the believing soul. David had a beautiful understanding of how God takes the believer and keeps him in the very hollow of His hand, in the secret of His pavilion, under the shadow of His wings, and under His very feathers. How much more can we, as born again Spirit-filled Christians count on the Lord to be all of these things to us? As long as we live in Christ, we can engage in the Almighty power of God to help us every day. The warning here is that we are to REMAIN in fellowship with the Lord in absolute surrender to His will. His power is with Him. Remember, it is His omnipotence that is needed in keeping your soul from the power of sin. Only God can do it. May we know what it is to walk step by step with the Almighty God as our Keeper.

Have you ever thought that in every action of grace in your heart, you have the whole omnipotence of God engaged to bless you? If your friend gives you a gift of money, you take it and go away with it. He has given you something of his. The rest of his money he keeps for himself. However, that is not the way it is with the power of God. God can part with nothing of His own power. Therefore, I can experience the power and goodness of God only so far as I am in contact and fellowship with Him. And when I come into contact and fellowship with Him, I come into contact and fellowship with the whole omnipotence of God. I have the whole omnipotence of God to help me every day.

A son has, perhaps, a very rich father, and as the son is about to begin a business, the father says, "You can have as much money as you want for your venture." All the father has is at the disposal of the son. And that is the way with God, your Almighty God. You can hardly take it in. Yes, His omnipotence is needed to keep every little worm that lives in the dust, and also to keep the universe. Therefore, His omnipotence is much more needed in keeping our souls from the power of sin.

Oh, if you want to grow in grace, do learn to begin here. In all your judgments, ponderings, thoughts, deeds, questions, studies, and prayers, learn to be kept by your Almighty God. What is the Almighty God not going to do for the child that trusts Him? The Bible says, "Above all that we ask or think" (Ephesians 3:20). It is God's omnipotence you must learn to know and trust. Then, you will live as a Christian was meant to live. Many may think that they live a godly life because they pray, tithe, go to church, occasionally read their Bibles, and are generally good people. How little we have learned to study God, and to understand that a godly life is a life full of God. It is a life that loves God, waits on Him, trusts Him, gives Him control of everything, and allows Him to bless it. We cannot do the will of God except by the power of God. God gives us the first experience of His power to prepare us to long for more, and to come and see all that He can do. God helps us to trust Him every day.

Thirdly, God's keeping is continuous. May we grasp the truth that our keeping by God is an all-inclusive, almighty keeping that is continuous and unbroken. People sometimes say, "For a week or a month God has kept me very wonderfully. I have lived in the light of His countenance, and I can say what joy I have had in fellowship with Him. He has blessed me in my work for others. But, it did not continue. It did not last." Oh, Beloved, why is it? Can there be any reason why the keeping of God should not be continuous and unbroken? Just think. All life is in unbroken continuity. God comes to us as the Almighty One, and without any condition He offers to be my Keeper. His keeping means that day by day, moment by moment, God is going to keep us. His keeping is continuous whether we are on the mountaintop, in the valley, or somewhere in between.

Consider the question, "Do you think God is able to keep you one day from actual transgression?" Many would answer, "I not only know He is able to do it, but I think He has done it. There have been days in which He has kept my heart in His holy presence. There have also been days when, though I have always had a sinful nature within me, He has kept me from conscious, actual transgression." Now, if He can do that for an hour or a day, why not for two days? Oh, let us make God's omnipotence as revealed in His Word the measure of our expectations. His keeping is continuous, but our obedience is up to us.

Will our God, in His tenderhearted love toward us, not keep us every moment when He has promised to do so? Oh Lord, let us once get ahold of the thought that our whole spiritual life is to be Your doing. Recall Philippians 2:13: "for it is God who works in you both to will and to do for His good pleasure." Once we get faith to expect that from God, God will do all for us.

God's keeping is continuous. Every morning God will meet you as you wake. He will give you the consciousness that through the day you have God to continually take charge of you with His almighty power. And, God will meet you the next day and every day. It doesn't matter if, in the practice of fellowship, failure sometimes comes. If you maintain your position of absolute surrender to God and say, "Lord Jesus, I am going to trust You day by day to keep me absolutely," your faith will grow stronger and stronger. You will know the keeping power of God in unbrokenness.

## Kept Through Faith

Now, for the other side: Believing. "Kept by the power of God through faith." How must we look at this faith? First, this faith means utter inability and helplessness before God. At the bottom of all faith there is a feeling of helplessness. If I have a bit of business to transact, perhaps to buy a house, the lawyer must do the work of getting the transfer of the property in my name and making all of the arrangements. I cannot do that work, and, in trusting that agent, I confess I cannot do it. And so faith means helplessness. In many cases it means I can do it with a great deal of trouble, but another can do it better. But in most cases, it is utter helplessness; another must do it for me. And that is the secret of the spiritual life. A man must learn to say: "I give up everything. I have tried and longed and thought and prayed, but failure has come. God has blessed me and helped me, but still, in the long run, there has been so much sin and sadness." What a change comes when a man is thus broken down into utter helplessness and self-despair, and says, "I can do nothing!"

Remember Paul. He was living a blessed life, and he had been taken up into the third heaven. Then the thorn in the flesh came, "a messenger of Satan to buffet me" (2 Corinthians 12:7). And what happened? Paul could not understand it, and three times he prayed to the Lord to take it away. But the Lord said, in effect, "No, it is possible that you might exalt yourself. Therefore, I have sent you this trial to keep you weak and humble." And Paul then learned a lesson that he never forgot: to rejoice in his infirmities. He said that the weaker he was, the better it was for him. For when he was weak, he was strong in his Lord Jesus (2 Corinthians 12:9-11).

Do you want to enter what people call "the higher life?" Then go a step lower down. There was once a man touring a factory. He was going to be escorted up to a tall tower to overlook some of the operations. The man came to the tower, entered by the door, and began going up the stairs. But when he had gone a few steps, the guide called out, "That is the wrong way. You must come down this way. Those stairs are locked up." The guide took him downstairs a good many steps, and there an elevator was ready to take him to the top. The man said, "I have learned a lesson that going down is often the best way to get up."

Ah, yes, God will have to bring us down very low. A sense of emptiness, despair, and nothingness will have to come upon us. It is when we sink down in utter helplessness that the everlasting God will reveal Himself in His power. Then, our hearts will learn to trust God alone.

What is it that keeps us from trusting God completely? Many say, "I believe what you say, but there is one difficulty. If my trust were complete and always abiding, all would come out right, for I know God will honor trust. But how am I to get that trust?" The answer is to stop living in the flesh. The great hindrance to trust in God is self-effort. So long as you have your own wisdom, thoughts, and strength, you cannot fully trust God. But when everything begins to grow dim before your eyes and you see that you understand nothing, then God is coming near. If you will bow down in nothingness and wait on God, He will become all.

As long as we are something, God cannot be all. His omnipotence cannot do its full work. That is the beginning of faith: utter despair of self, a ceasing from looking to man and everything on earth, and finding our hope in God alone.

Next, we must understand that faith is rest. In the beginning of the faith-life, faith is struggling. But, as long as faith is struggling, faith has not attained its strength. But when faith, in its struggling, gets to the end of itself, and throws itself upon God and rests on Him, then joy and victory come.

A great example of faith and rest in the Bible was when a nobleman came from Capernaum all the way to Cana to ask Jesus to heal his child. He implored Jesus to go with him so He could heal his child. When instead Jesus said, "Go your way; your child is healed" (John 4:50), the father rested in Jesus' word. He had no proof that his child was well and he had to walk back seven hours to find the truth. The father found out that his child was healed at the very hour Jesus spoke to him. That father rested on the word of Jesus and His work, and he went down to Capernaum to find his child well. He praised God, and he and his whole family became believers and disciples of Jesus Christ. Oh, friends, that is faith! When God comes to me with the promise of His keeping, and I have nothing on earth to trust in, I say to God: "Your word is enough. I am kept by the power of God." This is faith and this is rest. Can you rest on these words of our Lord?

It is a great thing when a man comes to rest on God's almighty power for every moment of his life. It is also great when he does so in the midst of temptations such as temper, haste, anger, unlovingness, pride and any other sin. It is a great thing in the face of these temptations to enter into a covenant with the omnipotent Jehovah - not on account of anything that any man says, or of anything that my heart feels - solely on the strength of the Word of God: "Kept by the power of God through faith."

Oh, let us say to God that we are going to prove Him to the very utmost. May we all pray, "Lord Jesus, We ask You for nothing more than You can give, but we want nothing less. My God, let our lives be a proof of what the omnipotent God can do. Let these be the two dispositions of our souls every day: deep helplessness, and simple, childlike rest."

Lastly, faith needs fellowship. Faith implies fellowship with God. Many people want to take the Word and believe it, but do not think it is actually necessary to fellowship with God. Ah, no! You cannot separate God from His Word. No goodness or power can be received separate from God. If you want to get into this life of godliness, you must take time for fellowship with God. People sometimes say, "My life is one of such hustle and bustle that I have no time for fellowship with God."

Ah! There is the need. Beloved friend, please remember two things. We have not been instructed to trust the omnipotence of God as a thing, and we have not been instructed to trust the Word of God as a written book. We have been instructed to go to the God of omnipotence and the God of the Word. Deal with God as that nobleman dealt with the living Jesus. Why was he able to believe the word that Jesus spoke to him? Because in the very eyes, tone, and voice of Jesus, the Son of God, he saw and heard something which made him feel that he could trust Him. And that is what Jesus can do for you. Do not try to stir and arouse faith from within. How often people have tried to do that, but to no avail! Leave your heart, and look into the face of Jesus. Listen to what He tells you about how He will keep you. Look up into the face of your loving Father, and spend time with Him every day. Begin a new life with the deep emptiness and poverty of a man who has nothing, and who wants to get everything from Him. Begin this new life with the deep restfulness of a man who rests on the living God, the omnipotent Jehovah. Try God, and see that He will open the windows of heaven and pour out a blessing so big that you will hardly be able to receive it.

Are you willing to fully experience the heavenly keeping for the heavenly inheritance? Robert Murray M'Cheyne, a Scottish preacher during the 1800's known for his godliness, and God's presence and power in his services, once said, "Oh God, make me as holy as a pardoned sinner can be made." If that prayer is in your heart, come now, and let us enter into a covenant with the everlasting and omnipotent Jehovah afresh. In great helplessness, but in great restfulness, let us place ourselves in His hands. And then, as we enter into our covenant, let us have this one prayer: that we may fully believe that the everlasting God is going to be our constant companion. Let us believe that He will hold our hand every moment of the day. He is our Keeper, watching over us without a moment's break. He is our Father, delighting to reveal Himself in our souls always. He has the power to let the sunshine of His love be with us all day. Do not be afraid that because you have your business you cannot have God with you always. Learn the lesson that the natural sun shines on you all day, and you enjoy its light. Wherever you are you have the sun - even if you can't see it or it is shrouded in clouds; God makes certain that it shines on you. And God will make certain that His own divine light shines on you, and that you will abide in that light, if you will only trust Him for it. Let us trust God to do that with a great and entire trust. Here is the omnipotence of God, and here is faith reaching out to the measure of that omnipotence. We can say, "All that God's omnipotence can do, I am going to trust my God for." Are not the two sides of this heavenly life wonderful? God's omnipotence covers me, and my will in its littleness rests in that omnipotence, and rejoices in it!

> Moment by moment I'm kept in His love;
> Moment by moment, I've life from above;
> Looking to Jesus, the glory doth shine;
> Moment by moment, Oh, Lord, I am thine![4]
> (Hymn by Daniel W. Whittle)

## Points to Ponder:

Being kept by the Lord is not about emotions. Good feelings are not necessarily an indicator of God's keeping you. Whether we are feeling happy or sad our Lord is still in control, if you are yielded to His will and trusting in Him alone. Likewise, circumstances are not an indicator of God's keeping. When we read the next verses after our reference verses in 1 Peter chapter 1, we see that while we rejoice in being "kept by the power of God through faith," we can experience various trials. Therefore, we see that God does not keep us from trials; He keeps us in them. The last two paragraphs of this chapter are overflowing with powerful truths of God's keeping. Spend some time with Jesus, the Lover of your soul, pondering and praying through these paragraphs. May you know Him anew as your Keeper. Let His love for you sink deep into your soul. It will change your life.

# CHAPTER 9

## *You are the Branches*

"I am the vine, you are the branches. He who abides in Me, and I in him, bears much fruit; for without Me you can do nothing." John 15:5

ANDREW MURRAY ADDRESSED THIS PORTION OF HIS BOOK TO CHRISTIAN workers. The great commission given to us by Jesus in Matthew 28:16-20 makes every believer a Christian worker. It does not matter if you are raising children to follow Jesus, pastoring a large congregation, or working in any job, "whatever you do, do it heartily, as to the Lord and not to men" (Colossians 3:23).

Everything depends on our being right in Christ. If I want good apples, I must have a good apple tree. If I care for the health of the apple tree, the apple tree will give me good apples. And it is just so with our Christian life and work. If our life with Jesus is right, all will come out right. Instruction, suggestion, help, and training in living a Christian life and doing Christian work or service has value. But, in the long run, the greatest essential is to have our full life in Jesus - in other words, to have Jesus Christ in us, working through us. Yes, there are many things to disturb us, or cause us anxious questionings. But, our Master has such a blessing for every one of us and such perfect peace and rest. He has such joy and strength if we can only come into, and be kept in, the right attitude toward Him.

"I am the vine, you are the branches." What a simple thing it is to be a branch; the branch of a tree or the branch of a vine. The branch grows out of the vine, or out of the tree, and there it lives and grows and in due time, bears fruit. It has no responsibility except to receive sap and nourishment from the root and stem. And if only we knew, by the Holy Spirit, about our relationship to Jesus Christ, our life and work would be changed into the brightest and most heavenly thing on earth. Instead of there ever being soul-weariness or exhaustion, our work would be like a new experience, linking us to Jesus as nothing else can. For, is it not true that often our work comes between us and Jesus? What folly! The very work that He has to do in me and I for Him, I take up in such a way that it separates me from Jesus. Many a laborer in the vineyard has complained that he has too much work, and not enough time for close communion with Jesus. He complains that his usual work weakens his inclination for prayer, and that his many conversations with men darken the spiritual life. Sad thought, that the bearing of fruit should separate the branch from the vine! That must be because we have looked on our work as something other than the branch bearing fruit. May God deliver us from every false thought about the Christian life!

Now, just a few thoughts about this blessed branch-life.

## Absolute Dependence

In the first place, being a branch is a life of absolute dependence. The branch has nothing. It just depends on the vine for everything. Absolute dependence is one of the most solemn and precious of thoughts. It has been said that absolute, unalterable dependence upon God alone is the essence of the religion of angels. It should also be that of men. God is everything to the angels, and He is willing to be everything to the Christian. If we can learn to depend on God every moment of the day, everything will come out right. You will receive the higher life if you depend absolutely on God.

Now, here we find it with the vine and the branches. Every vine you ever see, or every bunch of grapes that comes to your table, let it remind you that the branch is absolutely dependent on the vine. The vine has to do the work, and the branch enjoys the fruit of it. What has the vine to do? It has to do a great work. It has to send its roots out into the soil and hunt under the ground – often a long way out – for nourishment, and to drink in moisture. Then, its roots or stems turn the moisture and nourishment into that special sap which makes the fruit that is borne. The vine does the work, and the branch has just to receive the sap from the vine. The sap is then changed into grapes. The vine had the work to do, and the branches had just to depend on the vine and receive what it gave.

Is that literally true of my Lord Jesus? Must I understand that when I am called on to work, share my faith, pray in a group, etc., that all the responsibility of the work is on Jesus? That is exactly what Jesus wants you to understand. Jesus desires that in all your work the very foundation should be the simple, blessed consciousness: Jesus must care for all. And how does He fulfill the trust of that dependence? He does it by sending down the Holy Spirit – not now and then only as a special gift. But remember, the relationship between the vine and the branches is such that hourly, daily, unceasingly, the living connection is maintained. The sap does not flow for a time, and then stop, and then flow again. Instead, moment to moment, the sap flows from the vine to the branches. And just so, your Lord Jesus wants you to take that blessed position as a believer and as a worker. Morning by morning, day by day, hour by hour, and step by step – in every work – I have to abide in Him in the simple, utter helplessness of one who knows nothing. I must be as one who is nothing, and can do nothing. Oh, beloved, study that word nothing. Have you prayed and worshipped God in light of the fact that He is everything and we are nothing? Do you know the blessedness of the word "nothing"?

If I am something, then God is not everything; but when I become nothing, God can become all! The everlasting God in Christ can reveal Himself fully. That is the higher life. We need to become nothing. Someone has well said that the seraphim and cherubim are flames of fire because they know they are nothing, and they allow God to put His fullness and His glory and brightness into them. Oh, become nothing in deep reality, and as a worker, study one thing – to become poorer and lower and more helpless, that Jesus may work all in you.

Believers, here is your first lesson: learn to be nothing, learn to be helpless. The man who has got something is not absolutely dependent on God. But, the man who has nothing is absolutely dependent on God.

Absolute dependence on God is the secret of all power in your Christian work and walk. The branch has nothing but what it gets from the vine. We can have nothing but what we get from Jesus. "Abide in Me, and I in you. As the branch cannot bear fruit of itself, unless it abides in the vine, neither can you, unless you abide in Me. I am the vine, you are the branches. He who abides in Me, and I in him, bears much fruit; for without Me you can do nothing." John 15:4-5

## Deep Restfulness

Secondly, the life of the branch is not only a life of entire dependence, but also of deep restfulness. The little branch, if it could think, feel, and speak, and if we could say, "Come, branch of the vine, I want to learn from you how I can be a true branch of the living Vine," what would it answer? The little branch would whisper, "Man, I hear that you are wise, and I know that you can do a great many wonderful things. I know you have much strength and wisdom given to you, but I have one lesson for you. With all your hurry and effort in Jesus' work, you never prosper. The first thing you need is to come and rest in your Lord Jesus. That is what I do. Since I grew out of that vine, I have spent years and years, and all I have done is just to rest in the vine. When the time of spring came, I had no anxious thought or care. The vine began to pour its sap into me, and to give the bud and leaf. Likewise, when summer came, I had no care; and in the great heat, I trusted the vine to bring moisture to keep me fresh. And in the time of harvest, when the owner came to pluck the grapes, I had no care. If there was anything in the grapes not good, the owner never blamed the branch. The blame was always on the vine. Also, during the cold, dark winter, I had no care, for the vine still took tender care of me. And if you would be a true branch of Jesus, the living Vine, just rest on Him. Let Jesus bear the responsibility."

You say, "Won't that make me lazy? It will not. No one who learns to rest on the living Jesus can become lazy. The closer your contact with Jesus, the more the Spirit of His zeal and love will be borne in you. But, oh, begin to work in the midst of your entire dependence by adding to that deep restfulness. A man sometimes tries and tries to be dependent on Jesus, but he worries himself about this absolute dependence. He tries and he cannot get it. But let him sink down into entire restfulness every day.

> In Thy strong hand I lay me down.
> So shall the work be done;
> For who can work so wondrously
> As the Almighty One?[5]
> (Hymn by Eliza H. Hamilton; Handley G.C. Moule)

Beloved brethren, let's take our place every day at the feet of Jesus, in the blessed peace and rest that comes from the knowledge: I have no care, my cares are His! I have no fear; He cares for all my fears.

Come, children of God, and understand that it is the Lord Jesus who wants to work through you. You complain of the lack of fervent love. It will come from Jesus. He will give the divine love in your heart with which you can love people. That is the meaning of the assurance: "The love of God is shed abroad in our hearts by the Holy Spirit" (Romans 5:5); and of that other word: "The love of Christ Jesus constraineth us" (2 Corinthians 5:14, KJV). Jesus can give you a fountain of love so that you cannot help being loving according to knowledge and all discernment (Philippians 1:9-11). Rest in Jesus, for He can give wisdom and strength. You do not know how that restfulness will often prove to be the very best part of your message when sharing your faith. You plead with people and you argue, and they get the idea: "There is a person arguing and striving with me." But, if you will let the deep rest of God come over you - the rest in Jesus Christ, the peace, the rest, and the holiness of heaven - that restfulness will bring a blessing to the heart, even more than the words you speak.

## Much Fruitfulness

Thirdly, the branch teaches a lesson of much fruitfulness. The Lord Jesus repeated the word fruit often in this parable. He spoke first of fruit, and then of more fruit, and then of much fruit. Yes, you are ordained not only to bear fruit, but to bear much fruit. "By this My Father is glorified, that you bear much fruit" (John 15:8). In the first place, Jesus said, "I am the true Vine, and My Father is the Vinedresser" (John 15:1). God will watch over the connection between Jesus and the branches. It is in the power of God through Jesus that we are to bear fruit.

Oh, Christians, you know this world is perishing for lack of workers. And it lacks more than workers. Many workers are saying, some more earnestly than others, "We need not only more workers, but we need our workers to have a new power - a different life – so that we workers would be able to bring more blessing." Children of God, you know what trouble you take, say, in a case of sickness. You have a beloved friend apparently in great sickness, and nothing can refresh that friend so much as a few grapes. But, they are out of season. Still, what trouble you will take to get the grapes that are to be the nourishment of this sick friend!

And, there are people around who never go to church and so many who go to church, but do not know Jesus. And yet, the heavenly grapes – the grapes of the heavenly Vine – are not to be had at any price except as the child of God bears them out of his inner life in fellowship with Jesus Christ. Except the children of God are filled with the sap of the heavenly Vine, except they are filled with the Holy Spirit and the love of Jesus, they cannot bear much of the real heavenly grape. We all confess there is a great deal of work, a great deal of preaching, teaching, and visiting, a great deal of machinery, and a great deal of earnest effort of every kind. But, there is not much manifestation of the power of God in it. What is lacking? The close connection between the worker and the heavenly Vine is lacking. Jesus, the heavenly Vine, has blessings that He could pour on tens of thousands who are perishing. Jesus Christ, the heavenly Vine, has power to provide the heavenly grapes. But, "you are the branches," and you cannot bear heavenly fruit unless you are in close connection with Jesus Christ.

Do not confuse work and fruit. There may be a good deal of work for Jesus that is not the fruit of the heavenly Vine. Do not seek for work only. Oh, study this question of fruit-bearing. It means the very life, power, spirit, and love within the heart of the Son of God. It means the heavenly Vine Himself coming into our hearts.

You know there are different sorts of grapes, each with a different name. Every vine provides exactly that specific aroma and juice which gives the grape its particular flavor and taste. Just so, there is in the heart of Christ Jesus a life, a love, a Spirit, a blessing, and a power for men, that are entirely heavenly and divine, and that will come down into our hearts. Stand in close connection with the heavenly Vine and say, "Lord Jesus, nothing less than the sap that flows through You, nothing less than the Spirit of Your divine life is what we ask. Lord Jesus, I pray, let Your Spirit flow through me in all my life and work for You." Again, the sap of the heavenly Vine is nothing but the Holy Spirit. The Holy Spirit is the life of the heavenly Vine. What you must get from Jesus is nothing less than a strong inflow of the Holy Spirit. You need it exceedingly, and you want nothing more than that. Remember that. Do not expect Jesus to give a bit of strength here, and a bit of blessing there, and a bit of help over there. As the vine does its work in giving its own specific sap to the branch, so expect Jesus to give His own Holy Spirit into your heart. Then you will bear much fruit. Perhaps you have only begun to bear fruit, and are listening to the word of Jesus in this parable, "more fruit" and "much fruit." Remember, that in order for you to bear fruit, you just require more of Jesus in your life and heart.

At times, we can get into a dangerous condition of work, work, and more work. We pray over it, but the freshness, buoyancy, and joy of the heavenly life are not always present. Let us seek to understand that the life of the branch is a life of much fruit, because it is a life rooted and grounded in Jesus, the living, heavenly Vine. "I am the vine, you are the branches. He who abides in Me, and I in him, bears much fruit; for without Me you can do nothing." John 15:5

## Close Communion

Fourth, the life of the branch is a life of close communion. Let's again ask: "What has the branch to do? You know that precious, inexhaustible word that Jesus used: Abide. Your life is to be an abiding life. And how is the abiding to be? It is to be just like the branch in the vine, abiding every minute of the day. The branches are in close communion, in unbroken communion, with the vine, from January through December. And can I choose to live every day in abiding communion with Jesus, our heavenly Vine?

You may say, "But I am so occupied with other things." You may have ten hours of hard work daily, during which your brain has to be occupied with temporal things. God orders it so. But the abiding work is the work of the heart, not the brain. It is the work of the heart clinging to and resting in Jesus, a work in which the Holy Spirit links us to Christ Jesus. Oh precious reader, do believe that deeper down than the brain, deep down in the inner life, you can abide in Jesus, so that every moment you are free, the consciousness will come: "Blessed Jesus, I am still in You." If you will find time to put aside other work and to get into this abiding contract with our heavenly Vine, you will find that fruit will come. What is the application to our life of this abiding communion? What does it mean? It means close fellowship with Jesus in secret prayer. There are Christians who do long for the higher life, and who sometimes have received a great blessing. There are those who have at times found a great inflow of heavenly joy and a great outflow of heavenly gladness. Yet, after a time, it passed away. They have not understood that close personal communion with Jesus is an absolute necessity for daily life. Take time to be alone with Jesus. Nothing in heaven or earth can free you from the necessity for that, if you are to be happy and holy Christians.

Oh, how many Christians look on it as a burden and a tax, a duty and a difficulty, to often be alone with God. That is the great hindrance to our Christian life everywhere. We need more quiet fellowship with Jesus in prayer and in His Word. In the name of the heavenly Vine, you cannot be healthy branches – branches into which the heavenly sap can flow – unless you take plenty of time for communion with God. If you are not willing to sacrifice time to get alone with Him, and to give Him time every day to work in you and to keep up the link of connection between you and Himself, He cannot give you that blessing of His unbroken fellowship. Jesus Christ asks you to live in close communion with Him. Let every heart say: "Oh, Jesus, it is this I long for. It is this I choose." And, He will gladly give it to you.

## Absolute Surrender

Lastly, the life of the branch is a life of absolute surrender. These words, absolute surrender, are great and solemn. Perhaps we do not fully understand their meaning. But yet, the little branch preaches it. "Have you anything to do, little branch, besides bearing grapes?"

"No, nothing," the little branch replies.

"And now, what do you understand, little branch, about your relationship to the vine?"

"My relationship is just this: I am utterly given over to the vine, and the vine can give me as much or as little sap as it chooses. Here I am, at its disposal, and the vine can do with me whatever it likes."

Oh friends, we need this absolute surrender to the Lord Jesus Christ. And it is one of the most difficult points to make clear. It is also one of the most important and needful points to explain what this absolute surrender is. It is often an easy thing for a man or a number of men to come out and offer themselves up to God for entire consecration, saying, "Lord, it is my desire to give myself up entirely to You." That is of great value, and often brings very rich blessing. But the one question we ought to study quietly is: What is meant by absolute surrender?

It means that, as literally as Jesus was given up entirely to God, I am given up entirely to Christ. Is that too strong? Some think so. Some think that can never be. They cannot believe that just as entirely and absolutely as Jesus gave up His life to do nothing but seek the Father's pleasure, and depend on the Father absolutely and entirely, I am to do nothing but to seek the pleasure of Jesus Christ and to depend entirely on Him. But that is actually true. Christ Jesus came to breathe His own Spirit into us. He came to help us find our very highest happiness in living entirely for God, just as He did. Oh, beloved brethren, if that is the case, then we ought to say: "Yes, as true as it is of that little branch of the vine, by God's grace, I would have it to be true of me. I would like to live day by day so that Jesus may be able to do with me what He will."

Ah, here comes a mistake that lies at the bottom of so much of our own Christianity. A man thinks, "I have my business and family duties, and my responsibilities as a citizen. All this I cannot change. And now alongside all this, I am to take Christianity and the service of God as something that will keep me from sin. God help me to perform my duties properly!"

This is not right. When Christ came, He bought the sinner with His blood. I, who have been bought with the blood of Jesus Christ, have been bought to live every day with this one thought, "How can I please my Master?" Oh, we find the Christian life so difficult because we seek God's blessing while we live in our own will. We desire to live the Christian life according to our own liking. We make our own plans and choose our own work. Then, we ask the Lord Jesus to come in and make sure that sin will not conquer us too much, and that we will not go too far off in the wrong way. We ask Him to come in and give us so much of His blessing. But our relationship to Jesus ought to be such that we are entirely at His disposal. Every day, we are to come to Him humbly and straightforwardly and say, "Lord, is there anything in me that is not according to Your will, that has not been ordered by You, or that is not entirely given up to You?"

Oh, if we could wait patiently, I tell you what the result would be. A relationship between us and Jesus would spring up. It would be so close and so tender that afterward we would be amazed at how we formerly could have lived with the idea, "I am surrendered to Jesus Christ." We would feel how distant our fellowship with Him had previously been. We would understand that Jesus can, and does indeed, give us unbroken fellowship with Him all day. The branch calls us to absolute surrender.

Now, not so much has been spoken of about the giving up of sins. There are people who need that, people who have violent tempers, bad habits, and actual sins which they from time to time commit, and which they have never given up to the Lamb of God. I pray you, if you are a branch of the living Vine, do not keep one sin back. There are a great many difficulties about this question of holiness, and all do not think exactly the same with regard to it. This would be a matter of comparative indifference if only all are honestly longing to be free from every sin. Oh, that people would actually cry to God, "Lord, do keep me from sin!" Give yourself utterly to Jesus, and ask Him to do His very utmost for you in keeping you from sin.

There is a great deal in our work, in churches, and in our surroundings that we find in the world. It has grown all around us and we think that it is all right - that it cannot be changed. We do not come to the Lord Jesus and ask Him about it. Oh Christians, bring everything into your relationship with Jesus, and say, "Lord, everything in my life has to be in the most complete harmony with my position as a branch of You, the blessed Vine."

Let your surrender to Jesus Christ be absolute. It is difficult to understand that word surrender fully. It gets new meanings every now and then. It enlarges immensely from time to time. Nevertheless, let's all speak it out, "Absolute surrender to You, Jesus is what I have chosen." And Jesus will show you what is not according to His mind, and lead you on to deeper and higher blessedness.

In conclusion, this can all be gathered up in one sentence. Christ Jesus said, "I am the Vine, you are the branches." In other words, "I, the Living One who has so completely given Myself to you, am the Vine. It is impossible to trust Me too much. I am the Almighty Worker, full of a divine life and power."

You are the branch of the Lord Jesus Christ. If there is in your heart the consciousness that you are not a strong, healthy, fruit-bearing branch - not closely linked with Jesus, not living in Him as you should be - then listen to Him say, "I am the Vine; I will receive you. I will draw you to Myself; I will bless you. I will strengthen you; I will fill you with My Spirit. I, the Vine, have taken you to be My branch. I have given Myself completely to you; child, give yourself completely to Me. I have surrendered Myself as God absolutely to you. I became man and died for you that I might be entirely yours. Come and surrender yourself entirely to be Mine."

What shall your answer be? Oh, let it be prayer from the depth of your heart, that the living Jesus may take you and link you closely to Himself. Let your prayer be that He, the living Vine, will so link you to Himself that you will go away with your heart singing, "He is my Vine, and I am His branch. I want nothing more, now that I have the everlasting Vine." Then, when you get alone with Him, worship and adore Him; praise and trust Him; love Him and wait for His love. "You are my Vine, Jesus, and I am Your branch. It is enough; my soul is satisfied."

Glory to His blessed Name!

## Points to Ponder:

Jesus is enough. No matter what, Jesus is enough. Be much alone with God. "I am the vine, you are the branches" (John 15:5a). It's been a fabulous journey to absolute surrender thus far, and the adventure is just beginning! It's so exciting to think about what blessedness Jesus has for you next, Beloved!

# CLOSING PRAYER FOR YOU

Precious reader, we have prayed for you throughout your journey to absolute surrender to God. We know your path has been unique and tailor-made by Him for you and you alone.

Heavenly Father, We pray that your beloved child reading these words right now, continues to follow You on this exciting journey of absolute surrender day by day and moment by moment. May he/she hear Your voice more clearly, sense your presence more profoundly, and know your love more deeply. We also pray he/she has entered into the secret place of deep restfulness in Jesus, absolute dependence on You God, and that he/she lives every moment in the power of the Holy Spirit. Amen.

# END NOTES

1    Christianity Today Website. Available at https://www.christianitytoday.com/history/people/innertravelers/andrew-murray.html.

2    Refrain from the hymn, "Moment by Moment" written by D.W. Whittle during the 19th century.

3    "Aiden Wilson Tozer." AZQuotes.com. Wind and Fly LTD, 2021. 13 December 2021. https://www.azquotes.com/author/14750-Aiden_Wilson_Tozer

4    Refrain from the hymn, "Moment by Moment" written by D.W. Whittle during the 19th century.

5    Refrain from the hymn, "Oh, Give Me Rest From Self by Eliza H. Hamilton, 1869; My Savior, Thou Hast Offered Rest by Handley C.G. Moule, 1898. https://library.timelesstruths.org/music/Oh_Give_Me_Rest_from_Self/

# ABOUT THE AUTHOR

Over the past 25 years, Chris and Lisa have collaborated on a variety of ministries for women. They have chaired women retreats, taught Bible studies, and spoken at women's events. Early in her walk with the Lord, Chris was introduced to the writings of Andrew Murray. Since that time, she has made a point of teaching Andrew Murray's best known book, Absolute Surrender, to women in the many states in which she has lived. Each time, the women attending these groups proclaimed that this book enriched their relationship with the Lord Jesus by bringing them to a new level of intimacy, power, and communion never before experienced in their personal walks with Him. It is Chris and Lisa's greatest honor to bring this exciting adventure to you, dear sister in Christ. They know you will find the joy of surrender to be a precious treasure in your life, as they have experienced in theirs!